‘We think back through our mothers if we are women.’
—Virginia Woolf: ‘A Room of One’s Own’

For **Gerry**, **Martin** and **Chris**, and, of course, for **Dorothy**.

Deborah Delano

THE THINGS YOU DO

A Memoir

First publication

LEPUS BOOKS

2014

ISBN: 978-0-9572535-6-8

LEPUS BOOKS

lepusbooks.co.uk

Contents

Page

The Broken Arm

A Sunday afternoon and we'd been walking on the lanes and moors up towards Stoodley Pike, a huge phallic stone monument that dominates the skyline at the highest point between Todmorden and Hebden Bridge. The first snow had fallen and the day was bitterly cold under a diamond bright blue sky. It is a walk we do often, a climb up a steep wooded embankment and then a gentle path punctuated by farms and fields of sheep, like a Christmas card painting by Farquarhson: The Shortening Winter's Day.

We'd been larking about, duelling with fallen branches and ambushing each other with pine cone grenades. A drama was unfolding in the sky as ominous clouds started to appear from the north-east, eerily backlit by the low winter sun, like those about to disclose invading alien ships. More snow was coming.

We started our descent down a tarmac lane past a row of cottages, happily planning dinner and what to watch on telly that night. A scrawny boy of about ten was struggling to manoeuvre his sledge into a barn. My nosiness was my undoing because, fascinated by this mundane activity, I failed to notice a huge patch of sheer ice which had formed where a water tank had overflowed.

I went down in a comic book parody of slipping on ice and landed on my bent-back left wrist. I knew right away I had broken my arm and that our lovely simple day was annihilated. I took off my glove and, looking down at the injury, found my hand jutting at a horribly unnatural angle to my wrist. I knew I needed to stay focused on getting to Halifax A&E without fainting. I am a person known to faint at the merest cut finger and, though no blood was involved in this incident, the grotesque angle of my hand made pretty convincing fainting material.

Fortunately, the sledge-boy's mum and dad were at home with a handy four-by-four vehicle. Martine, my lover and fellow walking enthusiast, quickly took stock of the situation and, knowing my propensity to lily-livered behaviour, said: 'Don't look at it and don't faint.'

After a few moments of negotiations in which my dangling wrist and swaying motion figured as bargaining tools, it was agreed that the couple would take us home, from where we could make our own way to the hospital.

We shared the back seat with another small silent boy who stared gloomily at me. The journey down the most rutted road in all Christendom was agony, every bump sending excruciating pain ricocheting up my arm. Then, to add insult to injury, quite literally, our rescuers embarked on a 'domestic'.

Witnessing other peoples' marital discord is always disagreeable, but when trapped and injured in the back seat of their car it is intolerably oppressive—like being the children in a loveless failing marriage, your own fate entirely in their self-regarding and incompetent hands.

He asked her to get a blanket from the boot to rest my arm on and she (played by Alison Steadman) didn't like the tone of his voice and, we learned, was sick of how he spoke to her.

He responded by slamming the car to a stop (ouch!) and leaping out to get the entirely unwanted blanket. She confided to us when he was out of earshot that he'd been 'like that' lately. On his return, I carefully positioned the filthy rug beneath my swelling limb to forestall any recriminations and prayed they would find the self-control necessary to avoid further confrontation.

They got us home and we made for Halifax as fast as Martine's Clio could carry us in, what was by this time, a blizzard. In spite of my best efforts shock had set in and my whole body was shaking uncontrollably. After a wait among several other ice casualties, as well as quite a few where no injury could be ascertained save a tickly cough, we were seen by a nurse who whistled meaningfully through her teeth, like a car mechanic, and said they'd 'probly have to do summut about it.' I took this to mean 'summut' other than a plaster pot. The X-ray revealed that the wrist was broken at the base and a piece of bone had snapped off.

A young doctor (who looked about fifteen) reiterated the nurse's diagnosis. 'You'll have to go to Huddersfield,' he said. 'We only do children and gynaecology. If you can make your own way it'd help.'

'Okay,' I replied, imagining another perilous car journey with an arm not fit to be gazed upon by the faint of heart.

To my relief, there was further consultation between the young registrar and the orthopaedic surgeons at Huddersfield, and a decision was made that this snip of a boy would have to manipulate the arm to see if he could realign the bones, then plaster it and re-X-ray. He looked more horrified by the prospect than I did. A glut of similar incidents in the area had outstripped the capacity of the orthopaedics department to cope. We eyed each other in mutual horror, this young man and I. Another more senior Doctor joined us (he was about 18) and I was told to be brave while one pulled, the other pushed, and Martine administered gas and air. Never having given birth, it has taken me this long to fully appreciate the absolute uselessness of this analgesic. In fact, to name it such is to honour it far beyond its capability. Suffice to say, it was gut-wrenching agony.

To everyone's relief these young men did manage to manipulate my sorry limb into a better position and I was sent home in plaster with an appointment for the fracture clinic made for Tuesday morning.

At this appointment I was informed by the surgeon, a miserable old fellow lacking in even rudimentary social skills, that I would in fact need surgery, and at least six weeks off work. He glanced from Martine to me, and taking in our relationship with a kind of bemused disgust, was either unable or unwilling to answer any further queries. A kindly nurse had to explain the details to us. I've come across this sort before—male medical practitioners who have to be interpreted and mediated through female underlings.

I would have thought medicine to be a profession more in need of gifted communicators than monosyllabic misogynists.

I cannot help fantasise about a national health service that might exist in some parallel universe, where 'witch-finders' and sundry other religious zealots in an alternative middle ages had not, in the name of Christianity, wrested with ferocious violence the healing arts from the hands of wise women. Would it be different? I think it would.

So here I am. I've had the surgery. I'm off work. I'm wearing a plaster pot on my left arm. I haven't washed my hair in a week and I've exhausted every unread novel I can find as well as all the learned documentaries on my planner (now I know why I record them). I've got nothing left to do but write, with my remaining usable hand, some stories from my life. Why start with this business of the broken arm then?

Well, there is a connection...

On Being Born: 19th July 1958

Imagine, if you will, a council estate constructed in the early 1950's: solid brick-built houses attractively curving around a huge oval expanse of uninterrupted grass; streets named after rivers flowing in symmetry and occupied by those families lucky enough to have qualified, by dint of living in utter squalor, for the heretofore unheard of luxury of secure and sanitary housing for the working classes.

Every property featured a bathroom and indoor toilet, open lawns to the front and neat little fenced-off gardens to the rear. The estate won a prize for its design and at its heart stood a precinct of shops catering to every need of the 1950s family.

There was a butcher who made filthy jokes and gestures with sausages and slabs of liver for a receptive audience of housewives; a grocery store, where local news of illegitimate births, shotgun weddings and domestic beatings could be exchanged; a bakery, with its array of Eccles cakes, coconut Madeleines and individual fresh cream trifles served by a very dainty class of woman who forswore gossip of any kind; a post office, where people posted parcels to their more glamorous émigré relatives in Australia; a hairdresser who, it later transpired, was a closeted lesbian; and a hardware store with that smell now lost forever.

Today these shops are boarded up. They have fallen victim to the out of town superstores. The illiterate graffiti adorning the metal shutters advises: Fuk off wanka. The primary school closed down under Thatcher's 'on your bikes' economic strategies of the 'eighties. The streets and houses bear the ravages of unemployment, crime, drugs and alcohol abuse and, nestled among them, the government has cynically sited a refuge for asylum seekers.

The estate is called Kings Heath and it lies on the northern edge of Northampton, in the exact middle of England, and it is here that my family lived in a maisonette.

My mum had been given the key to a brand new house on the estate in 1952, but we moved from this spacious property with its own garden to the maisonette above the old people's flats. No one now knows why. It can only be supposed that my mum had fallen victim to one of the sort of sexual scandals to which she was occasionally prone.

By 1958 we were a family of five: my mum and dad, two sisters aged sixteen and eleven, and a brother, not quite seven. It was he, my brother Martin who, on this hot summers' day, fell while playing on the maisonette steps and, like his little sister fifty-two years later, stuck his arm out to break his fall. His arm went through the metal railings but he kept falling. My mother, when recalling the incident, as she did often, said 'Ooer, it were bent back like a banana.'

The sight of this disfigured limb precipitated an early labour and my mother retreated to her bed where she spent the remainder of the day screaming at ear-piercing decibels.

My dad, similarly prone to dramatic over-reaction, and believing my brother to have been a victim of violent attack, flew into a psychotic (I use this word advisedly) rage. This frequently preceded an epileptic fit, and indeed would have done so on this occasion had not my maternal grandmother the good sense and strength to thump him repeatedly on the back, while explaining the true nature of

Martin and Gerry *outside the maisonette - 1960*

the incident. This remedy proved efficacious and, sufficiently calmed, my dad was dispatched to the hospital with Martin on the bus.

My grandmother then proceeded to the birth, a rite she had performed on innumerable former occasions unencumbered by any qualification save experience and naked wit: a wise woman, to be sure. She was the sort of woman who rolled up her sleeves and got on with it. Much to her chagrin however, a midwife latterly arrived on the scene discharged and then debarred my grandmother from the labour room following a disagreement about the nearness of my arrival—years of know-how casually swept aside by modern medicine's march of progress.

When finally I arrived at 10pm that Saturday evening, I was strangling on my umbilical cord. The midwife had resolutely ignored my mother's pleas that I was imminent, and when I slithered into the world no scissors could be procured to sever the noose. This operation must eventually have been performed because I lived, though the emotional cord with which my mother bound me proved more difficult to disentangle.

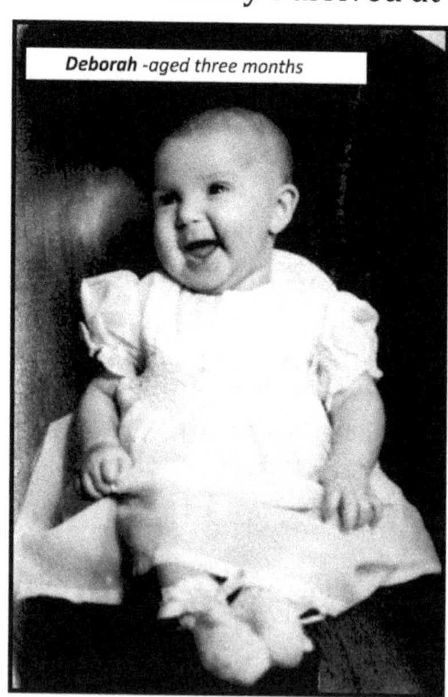
Deborah *-aged three months*

Most of the day's events have been described to me by my sister Gerry, then eleven years old. She and my cousin spent much of the day sitting on the stone steps outside the maisonette, kicking at dirt and listening to the screaming. At the news of my arrival they went door-to-door on the estate proclaiming my birth to the neighbours. Apparently no-one was very interested, and one woman slammed her door in their faces—no doubt someone my mother had wronged.

Later that night Martin crept into my mother's bedroom sporting his plaster cast.

'You've got a little sister,' Mum said and cuddled him to her.

'I'm still your only boy' he replied, burying his head in her neck.

Dorothy, My Mother

Dorothy was born in 1922 in Far Cotton, a random collection of streets and houses on the south side of Northampton that stretched away from the river Nene towards London.

I know little of any ancestry, and have to confess to an ambivalence of feeling towards the current preoccupation with genealogy. Connectedness to other people I measure through trust, respect and love. Sometimes this involves blood, but often not. My ancestors were probably pretty much like yours: some peasants who shagged each other and then struggled through lives determined for them by the whim of popes and kings.

Only two notable stories have come my way. One of them concerns an Anglo-Scottish love affair, at a time when such a thing was traitorous, resulting in a distant relative of mine riding on horseback from Scotland to England to marry his sweetheart. Hence my mother's Scottish maiden name, Munroe. The other, a startling coincidence; my maternal grandparents were both from families of eleven children, both in a boy/girl pattern and both with two years between each sibling. Stranger still, both families had had a twelfth child, little boys named Cedric who, unlike any other family member, had both been blond haired and blue eyed, and died at the age of two.

Dorothy - 1939

Dorothy's own childhood was poor but not unduly. She was the eldest of three siblings in a family probably best described as upper working class. Her father was a master carpenter who ended his career as a manager of a large timber yard and her mother was a housewife.

Dorothy had many maiden aunts – her mother's sisters – three of whom lived together as spinsters. Like many women whose hopes of love and marriage had been shattered by World War I they lavished their love, attention and hard-earned cash on their nieces and nephews. Dorothy was a particular favourite, and spent weeks and sometimes months living at their house where she enjoyed privileges and freedoms beyond the capacity of her parents.

The eldest of this trio was Aunt Nell who had been lumbered at eighteen with the onerous task of raising the rest of the family when her mother died, exhausted from continuous childbirth, at the age of forty-nine.

The youngest, Aunt Clare, had tragically lost her beloved, a promising young architect, not in the trenches but to cancer. He died three days before their wedding. She never recovered from the shock and grief.

The third, Aunt Flo, was a particularly straight-laced deaconess at the chapel in Kingsthorpe Hollow. She was always described as 'mannish', and was in fact a repressed lesbian. This became evident when the poor woman suffered a stroke in her seventies. Her brain was affected by the illness, and during her delirium she revealed a lifelong and deep sexual passion for the vicar's wife. A life, if ever there was one, determined by popes and kings.

What was distinctly odd about Dorothy was her waywardness and promiscuity. Her parents were hard working and upstanding citizens with a highly developed sense of propriety.

Her father in particular found her behaviour repugnant and openly favoured her sister who was a paragon of virtue. Dorothy strained against the leash of moral expectations. She was uncontrollable at school and a regular truant. At fifteen she ran away from home and hitchhiked to London with a lorry driver who she repaid with sexual favours. On another occasion, she was caught *in flagrante* in a shop doorway by the aforementioned Aunt Flo. This most fastidious of aunts was so undone with shock upon discovering that it was her own niece on the other end of the *al fresco* seeing-to that she made a small cry—and never mentioned the incident thereafter.

***My grandparents** - William and Fanny Munroe*

Dorothy was beautiful. A picture of her taken in 1939, which now stands on my mantelpiece, shows a young woman at the height of her physical charms. An almond face, full lips, a Marcel wave of luxuriant auburn hair, smiling deep brown eyes carefully framed beneath the perfect curve of her eyebrows. She had looked into the camera and seen a movie star looking back. It is little wonder that she entertained a string of boyfriends and admirers.

With one of these, Dorothy fell deeply in love. His name was Bill Boxall and he was a sergeant in the army.

Bill was handsome, self-assured and, at twenty eight, some 10 years her senior—a mature and steadying influence. To the delight of her parents, who were singularly relieved to have their troublesome daughter 'settled', the couple were engaged to be married in October 1940. A wedding was planned for her nineteenth birthday the following March. Bill courted Dorothy with perfect manners. He took her for drives in his borrowed army staff-car, and for evening walks around the town's Victorian parks—each proudly parading their enviable conquest. They went to the pictures twice a week and rounded off their night in the pub: a pint of best for Bill and a gin and IT for Dorothy. Every Sunday Bill spent with her family. He'd arrive promptly at noon with flowers for his prospective mother-in-law, chocolates for Dorothy's younger siblings, Bet and Frank, a firm handshake for her dad, and always some sought-after luxury item for his sweetheart.

***Dorothy** with siblings **Frank and Bet** - 1943*

Considering that the war was on, Bill was clearly a resourceful chap. One Sunday in late January, just six weeks before the wedding, Bill failed to arrive at noon. The family waited, postponing the dinner until the joint shrivelled and the Yorkshire puddings sank. Dorothy kept a vigil at the window, willing that his jeep had broken down, or that some vitally important military mission had come up to detain him. Bill didn't arrive that day, or the next. On Tuesday, a heavy knock came at their door, and two plain-clothes policemen asked to speak to Dorothy Munroe. Her anxious mother ushered them into the parlour and in sombre tones they explained that Bill had disappeared, along with £10,000 of the army's money. They enquired as to the seriousness of the relationship between them. Dorothy, in shock, was speechless; it was her mother who explained that they were to be married in March. Turning to Dorothy one of the dour policemen said 'In that case, my dear, we think he'll try to contact you. We want you to carry on as normal. Have you got a job?'

'Yes, officer,' she replied. 'I work at Lotus shoe factory.'

'Then we think he'll try to see you there,' he said. 'We'll be watching the factory.' And then, testing further, added 'Will you be a good girl and inform us if he gets in touch?'

'Yes, sir,' she volunteered in the glare of her parents' scrutiny. 'Of course I will.'

Dorothy waited, and days and weeks, then months, went by and Bill never reappeared. The only communication from him was an envelope post-marked London, addressed to her mother and containing £200 in crisp banknotes. This small fortune, which they dutifully handed in to the police, obviously part of the haul.

Dorothy never saw Bill again. Years later, when she told me this tale, I asked her if she would have turned him in to the law.

She laughed and said 'Would I heck. I'd have shouted: " 'Ere Bill, scarper." '

This disappointment sent Dorothy spiralling into the arms of the plethora of young servicemen stationed in and around Northampton. They were Americans, Irish, Scots—here today and gone tomorrow, maybe never coming back. By the following Autumn Dorothy realised with dawning horror that her period was late. The double standards of gendered sexual behaviour and the moral absolutes concerning sex outside marriage for women meant that either an illegal abortion or a husband would need to be found, and quickly.

First she tried remedies she hoped would produce spontaneous abortion. This was a doomed enterprise involving the insertion of slippery elm bark into the vagina. The drawing effect produced was supposed to induce abortion. It didn't. She also tried gin and hot baths. This too proved fruitless. Fearing the butchery of the back-street abortionist, she decided to pursue a husband instead.

She'd been dating an Irishman called David, a quiet, unassuming fellow who had made himself the brunt of derision in the pub by drinking orange juice. The Glaswegian squaddie leading this macho bullying was another of Dorothy's conquests, Jerry. In honesty, she was herself uncertain of the paternity of her unborn child. She had dated Jerry a couple of times but the relationship had fizzled out. She did though care deeply for the Irishman and decided she would tell him of her condition on their next date. Marriage had been discussed between them already and David had made clear that his intentions were honourable. Before they met again, though, war intervened and David was called into military action. She got a letter saying he'd be in touch as soon as he was back in Northampton. Dorothy knew that this would be too late. So she decided to 'swing it' on Jerry. She approached him with the news, which he greeted with denial and a flat refusal to marry her. There was nothing to do but involve her mother.

My grandmother, Fanny Monroe, was not a woman to trifle with. An interview between her, Jerry and his commanding officer produced little resolution to the problem but did provide her with the address of Jerry's own mother in Glasgow. It was to this good woman whom she appealed her case with a letter setting out the predicament and suggesting a marriage at the earliest possible time.

The Glaswegian matriarch replied by return of post agreeing entirely with Fanny's assessment of the situation. Possibly scenting a degree of stability and social mobility for her son, she also sent a letter to Jerry summoning him to Glasgow. Jerry feared his 'maw' and when she told him to 'Go awae back doon t'England and marry that wee lassie or ye'er no son o' mine,' that was precisely what he did.

The marriage was an ignominious affair. Dorothy's family were prepared to stand by her in the getting of a husband, but not to condone her sexual indiscretion with any sort of celebration. It was a bitter cold December day and Dorothy wore her best and newest dress and her old coat, made tolerable with a fake fox-fur trim. At three months, she wasn't showing physically but the tenor of the event left no one in any doubt as to its reason. Jerry wore the only set of clothes he possessed: khaki army-issue fatigues, overcoat and private's cap. They journeyed to the registry office on the bus, and a summary service was conducted under the judgemental eyes of town hall officials.

Dorothy *and* **Christine** *- 1943*
(taken to send to Jerry away at war

Afterwards, the few relatives in attendance left and the newlyweds went to the pictures. They were virtual strangers. Jerry let his new bride choose the movie. She chose 'How Green was my Valley' showing at the Gaumont—a melodramatic tear-jerker about a family struggling against the dramatic social changes wreaking havoc with their lives and their community. This was the heyday of Hollywood and John Ford's sentimental melodrama deftly underscores the value of hard work, family, sacrifice and inheritance—in short, Capitalist patriarchy. Its message: look, peasants, shut up and put up like these good folks, and you'll be rewarded in heaven.

The picture - or at least the cinema darkness - also gave Dorothy the chance she needed to sob her heart out.

After three days compassionate leave, Jerry was posted with the 8th Army into Monty's desert war. Dorothy would not see him again for four years.

Six months later Christine was born. Jerry wrote occasionally and sent watches and jewellery he'd stolen from Italian prisoners of war. Dorothy pawned this contraband, and with it funded a slightly more comfortable wartime lifestyle. She lived with her parents and worked, while her mother cared for the infant. Dorothy was free, notwithstanding the child and her parents' continuing disapproval, to pursue the interests of a young single woman; and this, of course, she did with enthusiasm.

David, the quiet Irishman, did return. He called for Dorothy two months after her marriage. She heard his voice at the front door, and her father explaining: 'Dorothy's married now son and she's having a baby, so you won't be able to see her again.'

This moment of pathos was a point, for Dorothy, on which her life turned. The possibilities of the past clanged shut behind her, leaving her locked in a future with Jerry Gibbons, the psychopathic Glaswegian.

The Gorbals Boy

Jerry entered this world two days after the armistice in 1918, arriving into that filthy urban mess created by industrial capitalism: the Gorbals district of Glasgow. He was christened William. This was an odd choice since the family was Catholic, although I think it likely that the average Glaswegian slum-dweller took a fairly pragmatic stance on religious affairs. The young William became known as 'Jerry' after a barefoot itinerant who roamed the district. William did not possess footwear of any kind until he was a working lad of ten, and this inauspicious nickname stuck.

Jerry was four when his father died. He had a brother two years his senior and two younger sisters. The family lived in abject poverty. They occupied a 'single end' in a tenement building. This was a room with a cavity bed and another shakedown bed. The girls shared the bed with their mother while Jerry and his brother shared the cavity bed. These beds, a common feature of the slums, were actually a cupboard in the wall with bedding inside. They shared a toilet with several other families who lived on the same landing, and a good many rats. There were no baths and they washed in the same solitary sink in which they performed every other task requiring the use of running water, and this included pissing.

***Gorbals Elementary School** - class of 1925*
***Jerry Gibbons** circled (only those with shoes sat at the front)*

The family eked out a living on government hand-outs known locally as the 'buroo' and the profits from Jerry's early criminal exploits. He thieved anything he could lay his hands on. A particularly lucrative stunt involved jumping onto the backs of the delivery lorries moving slowly through the tenement streets and throwing the load to his waiting cronies. When the driver caught on, the young villains would disperse like mice into the warren of alleys and closes. Jerry was small and athletic and always outran his pursuers. The booty would then be sold around the tenement closes and a tidy sum netted for the household purse.

His mother, the Maw, was a hard case. As an uneducated lone mother of four in a world lacking a welfare state her life choices were severely limited. Sober the rest of the week, on Saturday nights she went out for a 'wee dram' and came home fighting drunk. Like many of the tenement dwellers she chose the cheapest means of oblivion available: 'red biddy'. This was a potent mixture of cheap red wine and methylated sprits. Empowered by its lethal, brain altering properties, she stood in the middle of the street and issued a weekly challenge to the tenements.

'I'll fight ony fuckin' man that wants tae tek me oan, come oot yer hooses if ye fancy yer chances.'

Jerry and his siblings huddled together under the bed-bug ridden blankets and hoped no one took up the challenge.

The Maw also possessed an ability to spit with almost preternatural accuracy, and this was her favoured method of discipline. Jerry spoke of this gift with great reverence and indeed had inherited her skill. He tormented the teenaged Christine backcombing her hair in front of the living-room mirror. He would sit with his leg thrown over the arm of his chair, smoking and hissing deadly accurate

Woodbine spittle through his teeth. It never missed, and would hang, a viscous brown globule, from her stockinged leg. She clawed at the leg in disgust, sometimes ripping through the nylon. This inevitably provoked a fearful row, which he began by claiming that she 'Cudny tek a fuckin' joke,' and ended with his storming 'awae t'ma kennel' upstairs, declaiming that 'naebudy gaves a fuck aboot me in thus hoose.'

Jerry grew up in a world of grim and brutal violence. He worked as a barber's boy from the age of ten, supplementing the family income and helping himself to the cutthroat razors with which he fought in the neighbourhood. Razor fights were a feature of the Gorbals and boys wore their weapons hidden in lapel of their jackets. These ritualistic and often organised affrays were a bid for supremacy and reputation amongst a powerless underclass. The razors they used left victims scarred for life with what Jerry referred to as 'a sore face'. Jerry was a fearless battler, though his trademark weapon was not in fact his razor but his head. He boasted often of the men whose faces he'd split wide open by 'puttin' the heed oan.'

His teenage years of general thievery and mindless violence culminated in two years at her majesty's pleasure in the Barlinnie prison. He had been involved in a 'rammy' in which a young man had died. Whether he was himself the perpetrator, or just an enthusiastic participant, is lost to time, but the experience was sobering for the young thug. He was released in 1938 and, in an effort to avoid the life seemingly mapped out for him, he left his native Glasgow and went to London to find his fortune.

Jerry found a job in an engineering factory and a room to rent in Willesden. It didn't take very long though for him to establish criminal connections with a gang of con men. The bulk of his income during this time was gained through petty confidence tricks around the pubs and clubs of the capital. No doubt his willingness to violence was an aid in this new found career.

He enjoyed boasting about his criminal exploits, and on countless occasions regaled we children with these unedifying yarns. One such caper involved the sale of pornographic photographs of women.

'Ah wid go intae a pub an get natterin' tae some mug an ah wid let slip that ah'd got some dirty pictures in mah pocket that I widnae mind sellin'. Ah wid guv the chap a quick look. Aye, an' they were proper filthy pictures mind. Ah'd let oan that ah'd got tae get rid ayem an' he cud hov the lot fer three quid.'

Jerry would then demonstrate how he handed over the envelope of pictures from an imaginary breast pocket with a nimble back-hand pass. 'Ah wid tell him: "Don't open that in public mate, ye cud get three year fer that." ' And he'd chortle at the memory of his crafty dealings before revealing the lame denouement. 'Ah'd gi' the mug an envelope o' blank postcards. Oh aye, there's no flies on Jerry Gibbons, so there's not.'

Then war broke out and Jerry was called into action in the first week of hostility, obvious cannon fodder. The army still lacked weapons and uniforms but men like Jerry had always been in plentiful supply. He spent the next six years fighting a war against the fascist menace, although, ironically, his own attitudes bore close resemblance to that ideology. He was, for example, a white supremacist. Having speedily transferred his hatred of the Germans and the 'Japs' to black immigrants in Britain during the 1950's, he railed continuously against them and believed that the black races, unchecked by their white masters, would overrun 'civilised' society.

When he was in South Africa in 1943, a Scottish farmer had offered Jerry, were he willing to desert the army, a position on his extensive ranch as an overseer for the black 'workers'. Always one to spot an opportunity for gain through exploitation, Jerry seriously considered the offer. He later used his ultimate refusal as evidence of his commitment to his wife and child at home, though it seems more likely that he feared deserting the army. Men were jailed for this and Jerry's recent experience of prison was not one he would have been keen to repeat. He was also casually anti-Semitic, although he did admire the 'Jew boys' for their tenacious ability to remain solvent in the face of successive pogroms. Jerry was a man of his time and social class, and these views were commonplace. He was also, of course, deeply misogynistic. A woman's place was in the home serving her husband and any notion of equality between the sexes would simply never have entered his head.

Jerry spent the majority of the war in North Africa and the Middle East. He sustained one injury, not in combat but on his motorbike. He was a motorcycle messenger and he collided with an army truck, somersaulted over the handlebars and landed on his head on the bonnet of the lorry. Now, Jerry's head was particularly hard. He recovered after a few days in the military hospital and was discharged with no, visible at least, damage. Although it was later suggested that this accident could have caused the epilepsy from which he suffered for the rest of his life.

Jerry also came close to death on another occasion. He was on night patrol with seven comrades in the North African desert when a low-flying German bomber opened fire on them, strafing the sand with a blizzard of bullets. The eight men dived face down onto the sand as the attack raged overhead. Jerry stayed completely still in terrified silence until daybreak. When he finally stood up and began to move he realised that, while he had fallen into an indentation in the sand, all seven of his comrades-in-arms lay dead. He walked back to camp alone, hot tears stinging his face under the baking sun.

In 1990 the government sent Jerry five medals for his war effort. He put them on the coffee table lined up with his Woodbines and mug of tea and pondered them for a week. Then he parcelled them up and sent them back to the war office with a note explaining that they could stick them up their arse. This was a rare moment in my life when I truly admired him.

Jerry returned to Northampton at the end of 1945, to a wife still living with her parents and Christine, a child of four, who neither knew nor liked this invasive and perplexing stranger.

The Newlyweds

On Jerry's first night home Dorothy's parents offered to look after Christine so that the young couple could go out for the evening and renew their relationship. When they got to the end of the street Dorothy asked her new husband where he'd like to go.

'Ah'm awae fer a drink wi' mah pals. Ye can fuck off an' earn some money, I'll meet ye back here at hof pas' eleven,' was his even reply.

Stunned, Dorothy watched him walk away up Kingsthorpe Hollow towards the town and wondered what to do next. She could not return to her parents, own the truth and beg them to help her put right this terrible mistake she'd made. The shame would have been too great and their disappointment too much of a burden. This action would throw her onto the mercy of her father, and his sanctimonious attitude and bald dislike of her would have been even less appealing, and certainly more controlling, than her marriage, however flawed.

Dorothy walked for some time, trying to elucidate her feelings and to grasp the parameters of the life that lay before her. Finally she went into a pub and ordered a Port and Lemon. A woman alone in a pub was not, at the time, a common sight and she was quickly joined by an American air force officer. He bought her a couple more drinks and then invited her back to his rooms. There he cooked a meal of 'ham and eggs', which they shared. He was kind to her and he did not ask for or expect sex. Dorothy told him her story.

'Honey, a nice girl like you deserves someone better,' he sympathised. They spent the rest of the evening talking and at 11.15 he walked her back to her meeting place, and there he left her, to wait alone in the empty street.

Jerry turned up at midnight, drunk and demanding his share of any money she had made. When she told him how she had passed her evening he told her she was a 'fuckin' mug' and that she was 'sittin' on a gold mine'. This was one of Jerry's favourite expressions and one he cheerfully used to express the obvious good fortune that women held, to make easy money, in the simple possession of a vagina.

In the months that followed the newlyweds arrived at a détente. Jerry got a job at Barratts shoe factory, and with this and the money Dorothy had put aside from his wartime plunder they scratched together the deposit to rent a house. It was a small dilapidated terrace six years away from demolition. They continued their eccentric social life, with Jerry preferring the company of his pals and Dorothy making her own entertainment. Sometimes she went to the 'pictures'. There were nine thriving cinemas in the town at the time and Dorothy lived out her dreams under their luminescent screens. Her favourite stars were Barbara Stanwyck, Bette Davis, Joan Crawford, Lana Turner and Susan Hayward—fabulous women and spellbinding actresses, Dorothy was entranced by the power of their magic art.

Dorothy also increasingly went to pubs. She was, at twenty four, still unbearably lovely and she met, and spent evenings with, an array of male 'friends'. Sometimes, these men gave Dorothy gifts, often of money. Jerry was perfectly happy with this arrangement. Eventually the couple began to enjoy evenings out together more often. Occasionally, they would befriend a lone male in the pub and at the end of the evening's socialising Jerry would conveniently disappear leaving his wife to develop the acquaintance. Dorothy had always enjoyed the company of men and she revelled in the attention they gave her. The dubious morality of the situation occurred to neither of them. The only potential problem for Dorothy was being found out and talked about locally. For Jerry, like many raised in poverty, this behaviour was simply everyday existence.

Meanwhile, Dorothy's parents continued to care for Christine. This allowed Dorothy to continue working at

Lotus shoe factory. Jerry was unhappy with this situation. He loathed Dorothy 'working'. He thought a man should keep his wife and despised men who 'let' their wives work as weaklings, or 'Jew boy' money grabbers—the irony of this contradiction seemingly lost on him. Also, Christine disliked him intensely and refused to run to greet him when he came home from work as he expected. As his discontent grew they decided to 'go in for' another child and Dorothy fell pregnant again by March of 1946. She left her full time employment and they managed on his wage and her 'supplementary' income.

Jerry and Dorothy - 1952

Jerry wanted a boy, of course, but another little girl arrived and they named her Geraldine, or Gerry for short, after her dad. He doted on the infant. Christine, who had for five years been an idolised only child living largely with her grandparents, was moved into a bedroom of her own. She suffered a mental breakdown. This wasn't the term used at the time but her symptoms – insomnia, fearfulness, hysteria and refusal to eat – seem to suggest this diagnosis. Similarly, the remedy offered by the Doctor recognised the emotional nature of the child's malady. He suggested that they move her into the parental bedroom and ensure that they lavished the same amount of attention on her as they did on the new baby. Dorothy acted at once on these instructions and Christine gradually improved, though she harboured a jealous antipathy towards her sister which persisted well into adulthood.

Dorothy - 1952

Gentlemen Callers

During the austere years after the war Dorothy deepened her already close bond with her sister, Bet. She too had married and become a mother, and the two families lived in close proximity. Bet looked a lot like Dorothy, but a somehow paler, more insipid version. Bet was pretty enough but Dorothy had purloined all the glamour in their genes. The sisters spent every day together, nursing and walking their babies, deciding what to cook for their respective husband's dinners, shopping, eating cakes when their meagre ration books allowed and sharing intimacies.

Bet was Dorothy's confidante and privy to her peculiar marital arrangement. She detested Jerry and encouraged Dorothy to leave him.

Bet and **Dorothy** - *1951*

This antipathy between the in-laws was only heightened when Jerry made a pass at Bet. He had asked if she 'fancied her hat knocking off' while attempting to put his hand up her skirt. She was horrified and reported the incident to her sister. Dorothy was sympathetic and promised to remonstrate with Jerry, though in fact she simply stored the information in her armoury of tactics with which to outflank him in future quarrels. Herein lay the essential difference between the sisters. Dorothy was worldly and sexually sophisticated and she carefully protected her beloved sister's guileless innocence.

Dorothy continued to have many male 'friends'. Mostly they were men she and Jerry had met on their Saturday evening pub crawls round Northampton's insalubrious watering holes. These men were, more often than not, foreign. Some of them were white Europeans and some of them were black. At this time racial mixing was considered a social evil, and white women who slept with black men were regarded as prostitutes. It cannot have escaped Dorothy's awareness that her conduct was outside the bounds of social norms. This did not stop her from pursuing such relationships. It was as though the socialisation process reinforcing racial prejudice and sexual abstinence for women had somehow failed, with Dorothy, to stick. Neither did Jerry's racism stand in their way. In fact, I suspect that the sexual psychology that surrounded their marriage was only enhanced by such liaisons.

Sometimes Dorothy entertained men during the day when Jerry was at work. This was difficult for him to keep tabs on. Bet could always be relied upon to aid Dorothy in any enterprise which might attenuate her marriage and she minded the children. Dorothy had two regular callers, both Polish: one a Jew called Ziggy and the other a Catholic, called George. These gentlemen callers were generous to Dorothy and they provided extra cash for groceries. Jerry kept the bulk of his wages for himself, apportioning a few pounds housekeeping to Dorothy each week. The money she made was essential to feed and clothe herself and her children. Such has been the nature of prostitution for time immemorial.

Bet and Dorothy
Margate - 1950

When Dorothy fell pregnant again at the beginning of 1951, she was panic-stricken. She was reasonably certain that the father of the child was George, the Pole, but she could not rule out Moses, one of the black men she had slept with. If the baby was born black her parents and the world would know what she'd been up to. The pregnancy was fraught with this secret knowledge. Dorothy knew that, if her fears came to pass, she alone would shoulder the burden of shame. Jerry's part in this travesty would have been that of cuckolded husband. The 'adulterous wife' explanation would have been much more palatable for society to digest, than the complicated truth.

When the child was born, a boy, he was not in fact black, but blue. He had a mild case of cyanosis, a disease caused by a lack of oxygen in the blood stream. This condition, and the stress of the pregnancy, led Dorothy to a period of post-natal depression during which she was unable to care for her newborn son, or even touch him. She was racked with misery and guilt. Bet cared for the child as Dorothy's despair deepened. Then, three months later, Dorothy awoke one morning cured. She raced to Martin's cot and held him to her and from that moment on adored him with a fervour that engulfed her very being.

Bert (I)

Every Tuesday night Dorothy and Bet went to the pictures. The husbands 'babysat' for the children. It's an indictment of the state of gender equality that I still hear women today talking about their husbands 'babysitting' for their own children. In the 1950's the 'new man' was still decades away.

The sisters spent their freedom wisely, they bought toffees from the newsagents and caught the bus to town in time to catch the Pathe news and the B feature. They started on the sweets on the bus, and one night as they passed the bag between them, a hand reached over from the seat behind and pinched a toffee.

'Oi y'cheeky sod,' Dorothy exclaimed as she slapped the hand away.

'Where are two beautiful young women like you off to on a Tuesday night,' the interloper replied. He was smartly groomed and well-spoken, with an ambiguous foreign accent and a big, distinctly hooked nose. Dorothy, always susceptible to a compliment, explained that they were going to the pictures. The man introduced himself as 'Bert' and by the end of the bus ride the new friends had decided to spend the rest of their evening together. Bert paid for the tickets and the drinks they had afterwards, and at the end of the evening he asked if they'd be on the same bus next week.

Bert worked at the government buildings, and over the following months he established a fraternal friendship with Bet and, no surprises here, became Dorothy's lover. The nearness of his offices to our house meant that he spent most of his 'coffee breaks' with her. He was, he said, French and had come to England during the war escaping the Nazi occupation of Paris. He was married to a wife whom he did not love and had two children. Gradually he became a kind of family friend. Gerry, my sister, was taken out for tea and cakes with him in the afternoons when, much to her discomfort, he played 'footsie' under the table with Dorothy. In retaliation, she called him Captain Hook behind his back on account of his nose.

Unlike many of Dorothy's men friends Bert didn't have any kind of relationship with Jerry. In fact he detested Jerry and did all in his power to get Dorothy to leave him. With four children and a husband who, though not sexually possessive, simply saw her as his property, this would have been a difficult move to make. Bert certainly had no intentions of leaving his wife and, while she enjoyed his attentions and friendship, being tied to him as a kept mistress was not a life Dorothy could contemplate. Bert was a demanding and outré lover and though this was diverting on a casual basis it would have proved irksome for her as his dependent.

***Dorothy** - 1953*
Bet's bike at roadside

Bert was also a good friend to Dorothy, and when her sister Bet was diagnosed with terminal cancer at the cruel age of thirty five he helped her to live through the tragedy of her death. This she did, but I never heard my mother talk about her sister without tears, often prompted by the recounting of some absurd misadventure they'd shared. It was this laughter that had epitomised their love for each other.

I spent much of the first year of my life in Bet's sick room as my mother nursed her dying sister. Bet, at times, was strong enough to look after me alone while Dorothy did the shopping and cooking for the two families. I was just 14 months old when Bet died leaving Dorothy bereft of her best friend and confidante. As I grew, I came to inherit this role on which she so depended.

The Other Spencer Estate

Deborah - *outside the maisonette, 1960*

I was named by my sister Chris, whose passions had been inflamed by Burt Lancaster and Deborah Kerr rolling about in the surf in 'From Here to Eternity'. My first memory is of moving from the maisonette—where the stone steps that had initiated Dorothy's labour had proved back-breaking with a Tansad pram and a baby. It was 1960 and I was 2 years old and desperate to ride with my dad and brother in the removal van. Instead I was made to go with my mum on the bus. We stood in the drizzle as the van went by with my brother waving spitefully from the window.

The house we moved to was on Spencer Estate—so named for the illustrious Althorpe family who had bequeathed the land. It was less than a mile from the maisonette on Kings Heath but much less salubrious. Swapping a maisonette for a house wasn't easy so Mum took what she could get. Some of the people on the estate were smelly and lived in houses that reeked of cold grease. Others had sex with close relations. If this were a Venn diagram there would be several in the overlap.

When we arrived at our house that day, Mum realised that the ceilings were all shabbily painted dark blue, and some of the brush strokes had crept down the wall, giving the place a prescient air of gloom. No one could understand why she hadn't noticed this suicidal décor when she inspected the property, but in her desperation to move she probably didn't look up. And empty houses always look bleak. At the sight of it Mum went into a paroxysm of hysterical screaming and Dad blacked her eye to calm her down. It worked. He didn't hit her often but when he did, it was to mark the end of their dialogue, a full stop to an outrageous sentence. Violence was Jerry's dominant emotional response. He never beat her up. It was always a single punch and a black eye. This happened, probably, six times during my childhood, and though it was frightening, the hysteria was more emotionally damaging. I didn't need him but I needed her, and in her temporary incoherence she wasn't there in any sense I could hold on to. So the violence made him the villain and that fitted neatly into my understanding of the world.

***Deborah** sporting a new bonnet*

Margate

We were poor, but not as poor as a lot of the families on the estate. One thing that marked us out as better off was our week at the seaside. Every year during the factory fortnight we got the coach to Margate. I suffered excessively from travel sickness and spent the six-hour journey with my head in a bag wishing to die. There were few motorways at the time and the roads were tortuous.

We had full board in 'Mary and Tom's' guest house—breakfast, dinner and tea were included, and we managed to fit in supper in a café. Self-catering in a caravan would have been cheaper but my mum said, 'That's no bloody holiday for a woman.'

Deborah and **Martin** - *Margate 1962*

Dorothy, Deborah & **Christine** - *Margate 1968*

Deborah *finds a random lap*

Deborah, Dorothy & Jerry *(failing to amuse me)*

Every day we went to the beach and hired deckchairs from a saucy vendor who usually had some banter with my mum. Dad didn't join us until later. He always spent the first hour of the day in the public lavatories on the front 'having a quiet shit' and reading his paper. I built sandcastles and pestered my brother and whichever friend he'd been allowed to bring along to play with me. Usually any glimmer of interest I mustered from them would mean my being buried in sand up to my neck and having my head used for target practise. When they got bored with this amusement they went to the arcades on the front to play bingo and slot machines, entertainments forbidden to me.

Sometimes we played Putting, and on one memorable occasion Mum let out a long and staccato series of farts, another blast emitting with each step. Dad was furious because other people on the green might have heard and he barked his disapproval: 'Ye rotten arsed swine, ye are.'

I was doubled up, howling with mirth, and Mum actually compounded the crime by then wetting herself with laughter. Whenever she laughed a lot she'd have to cross her legs because her bladder was weakened by having four kids.

It is hard to distinguish real memories from photographs. The photographs I have reveal something like Weegee's famous Coney Island crowd: a black and white sea of the proletariat. There's my mum, plumper by now but still looking glamorous in bathing suit and sunglasses; Martin and his mate in matching cowboy hats; me with protruding bony ribs and football raised aloft; my dad, Woodbine in hand, pulling his stupid 'photo face'. These images have fused with my memory, but two things have resonated down the years from Margate beach. I was given a 'tanner' to spend on ice-cream and I dropped it in the sand. My frantic searching was hopeless and, knowing the scarcity of the holiday budget, I pretended to my mum and dad that I'd eaten my icy at the van to stop it melting. I didn't care about the ice-cream I just wanted them to feel they'd made me happy. The other memory was my dad arriving at the beach from his sojourn in the toilets and showing Mum the front page of his paper.

'Oh no!' she cried out. 'Poor Marilyn's dead.' And then she actually wept.

Marilyn Monroe

When I first became properly aware of Marilyn I was shocked. Mum and I were watching 'Niagara', curled up together on the settee. I must have been eleven, and I was outraged by the scene where she plays 'Kiss' on the gramophone and sways in a kind of sexual trance in rhythm with the music. Of course I found her mesmerising, and yet horrifying at the same time. By the time we got to the scene where she walks in a skin tight dress across a cobbled street, and the camera follows fixated on her arse, I was literally rolling about on the floor, holding my head saying

'Oh my god, how could she do that.' My mum thought I was funny to be so moved by the scene.

'She's Marilyn,' she said, as though that was explanation enough.

I was at once appalled and delighted by Marilyn's sexual presence, though at the time I had no clever analysis, just raw emotion and something quite close to anguish.

After that I saw every Marilyn movie I could, and I read and re-read Fred Lawrence Guiles biography of her, the only one that was around at the time. I have never connected my love and admiration for Marilyn with my lesbianism but more with my nascent feminism. It was the objectification of her body that so disturbed me. This was a body upon which thousands of years of misogyny seemed to crystallise.

She was an averagely pretty, unloved, adopted, pillar-to-post little girl called Norma-Jean, ripe and ready to be created and re-designed as Marilyn Monroe, the sexiest woman in the world. How can anybody be that? Oppression and abuse were played out in her personal life and simultaneously on the screen in a succession of exploitative films culminating in 'The Misfits'.

This vehicle, written especially for her by her husband at the time, Arthur Miller, has her run screaming into the desert pleading with men to stop killing. Miller's insight is gruellingly accurate and the shooting of the scene provoked a breakdown for Marilyn. A man she loved and trusted provided a narrative on which this vulnerable and drug-addicted victim of patriarchy impaled herself.

On set, the director, John Huston – another man she revered – called her a whore. Marilyn plays a fragile divorcee caught up in a triangle of damaged men. She eventually sleeps with one of them, 'Gay', played by Clark Gable. As a child, Marilyn had made Gable her fantasy father. It would prove to be the last film for both Monroe and Gable. Gable died five days after shooting ended and his widow held Marilyn responsible due to the stress created by her lateness on set. So, she has sex with her father figure, then kills him in a bizarre confluence of fiction and reality—Freud's Electra and Oedipus complex realised in a moment where the divine fiction of Marilyn Monroe runs headlong into, and ultimately destroys, the sorry little every-girl Norma Jean.

It goes without saying that I did not have the analytical faculty to draw any such conclusions at the time I was rolling on the floor, watching Niagara in an agony of love and embarrassment. Yet, my emerging feminism is the most satisfying explanation for the sudden violence I experienced, because something about the medium of film and its use to demonise, categorise and humiliate women became completely apparent to me, though I had no language then to express it. Of course I experienced the sexual objectification on a visceral level – you'd have to be dead not to – but something else happened. This was where my 'personal' got 'political'.

This same visual technology, now aided by the information superhighways, has allowed the pornography industry – the cultural expression of globalized capitalism – to spread exponentially. Liberation from capitalist patriarchy has never been a more pressing issue as women are stoned to death for adultery in the middle-east and trolls on the internet vilify and abuse women trying to engage in intelligent debate.

In Marilyn I could see that the very things that made women successful and desirable were the things that would be used to destroy them. Catharine Hakim, the anti-feminist writer, in her recent diatribe on 'erotic capital' makes the point that women who are beautiful are more successful and that they should capitalise on their virtues. Marilyn Monroe possessed more 'erotic capital' than anyone who ever lived and look where it got her. My Mum had loads of erotic capital and it made her a whore. When we get sex (erotic) mixed up with power and money (capital) all women get is fucked.

Flowering Currant

When people ask me when I first knew I was a lesbian I'm never sure what to say. We are trapped in symbol and language, so the answer would have to be that it was not until after I knew such a category existed. But I knew I loved women, and I knew I had sexual responses to other girls from the age of four. I had numerous sexual encounters with boys—commonplace on Spencer estate among the grubby children. These were usually of the 'I'll show you mine' variety. But I also had a sexual relationship

Deborah - aged five

with another girl of a different kind altogether. Jane was two years older than me and my first chosen friend. I looked up to her and adored her and we had sex. We touched each other and came to orgasm. I don't know if this is common since not one word of sense is ever spoken on the subject of childhood sexuality, but I began having orgasms before I went to school. We did it in her garden shed, in the thicket of trees near the bus stop and on the wasteland before they built the centre for the disabled. To this day I cannot smell a flowering currant bush without being transported to those hot summertime trysts.

Jane lived on the other side of our street and her dad was one of the only people on the estate who had a car. Her mum was stark raving mad. She always seemed a kind person to me, but when her madness was upon her she did terrible things. One day she ran up the street wearing nothing but a sanitary belt and soiled towel. All the adults agreed that it would have been better if she'd just been naked.

It was possibly this that branded Jane as a bit of an outcast, like me. I was always on the edge of the gangs of kids that hung round the streets, partly because I feared them and partly because my mum was regarded with suspicion and jealousy by the other mothers. Her 'callers' did not go unnoticed and, as the '60s progressed, neither did her miniskirts. As I sat on the kerb one day outside Jane's house waiting for her to come home from school a neighbour came out and told me to clear off, needlessly adding 'And yer mothers an old 'ow d'yer do.'

I understood this to mean prostitute and my heart leapt into my throat in a painful lump. I felt as though my relationship with Jane was somehow part of this sexual incontinence, and that everyone knew. Whatever innocence I may have once had was lost. Sex was furtive and wrong and all messed up with morality and judgement.

My relationship with Jane continued until we moved house again when I was nine. I missed her for a time but as we grew older the general 'wrongness' of our relationship had marred its simple delight.

I did see her once more after that time, as an adult. I was walking hand-in-hand with my girlfriend and her two children in the park. I recognised Jane at once, she too was with children and she tried to avoid my eye. I went up to her and said, 'Hello, Jane. Do you remember me? I'm Debbie Gibbons.'

Jane looked awkward and pretended she'd just seen me. She'd married a soldier and had two kids and she was moving to some overseas army camp. Her homophobia was palpable, and when I pointed out my girlfriend and the children it was as if I'd said: 'We used to have sex in the long grass,' rather than 'That's my partner and her kids.'

Poor woman.

HELP!

In these first few years of my life music became and remains central to my being. It was the place I escaped to, where I lived out my fantasies and where I began to create myself. My older brother and sisters bought a new single every week and we had a stacking radiogram to play them on. I stood behind the settee where I was too small to be seen and danced and sang my heart out to 'The Wanderer' by Dion, 'Runaway' by Del Shannon and 'I Don't Know Why I Love You (but I do)' by Clarence (Frogman) Henry—and to this I did the gravelly voice, too. I wanted to play the piano but ambitions such as this were unheard of on Spencer Estate.

When Martin was given The Beatles LP 'HELP' for his fourteenth birthday it became the first soundtrack to my life. We played it every morning while we were getting ready for school and I knew every track off by heart. My favourite, somewhat portentously, was 'Hey, You've Got to Hide Your Love Away'. I didn't know it at the time but this was John Lennon's homage to their homosexual manager, Brian Epstein. This is the song that played in my head as I walked to school throughout the winter of 1965.

We were all into music. It was the time when teenagers went screaming mental over pop stars and our Gerry used to 'rip up cushions' over Billy Fury and, hard though it may be to stomach, our cousin did likewise over Cliff Richard. I don't think they ever actually ripped a cushion – my dad would have gone mad if they had – but they tore at them in a kind of frenzy of unrequited sexual energy.

I bought my first single when I was 10, out of a ten-bob note given to me by Polish George, my Mum's friend. It was Nina Simone's 'Ain't got no, I got life'. I felt sure it was all about me. My first album was Motown Chartbusters Volume 3 with the space age silver sleeve and, as my teenage angst started to kick in, I bought 'Ladies of the Canyon'—and so began my lifelong worship of Joni Mitchell. I spent much of my teenage life lying on my bedroom floor, escaping into her progressively luminous albums, smoking Silk Cut cigarettes. In 'Judgement of the Moon and Stars (Ludwig's Tune)', she sings:

It's the judgement of the moon and stars
Your solitary path

Draw yourself a bath
Think what you'd like to have for supper

I loved the hugeness of the 'judgement' set against the prosaic nature of human existence; Joni Mitchell made me feel less lonely in the world.

Getting Dad Out of the Oven

During the years in the Spencer Estate house, Dad's drinking increased, and so did his epileptic fits. This affliction had emerged soon after he came back from the war, though to begin with they were mild. He would stare into space for several minutes, then continue whatever he was doing completely unaware of any lapse. Sometimes, he'd say random things that didn't make sense, and minutes later have no recall of having done so. More frequently during this period he actually fell down foaming at the mouth, and this seemed to happen more when he was drunk.

He would not accept that he was epileptic and he eschewed any kind of medical intervention. In Jerry's book real men didn't get sick, and if they did, they gargled in Condy's Crystals and got on with being a hard case. 'Condy's Crystals' were some sort of drain-cleaning product that he'd bought home from his years in the desert during the war. He regarded them as a panacea for all ills. No one in our house ever admitted to any kind of illness within his earshot, for fear of being forced to gargle with this poison.

When drunk, his mood was entirely unpredictable. Sometimes he'd come in and play Jimmy Shand's Scottish reels while performing a highland fling and, grim though this was, it was preferable to the times he came home and tried to kill himself. His favourite method was putting his head in the gas oven. Usually this happened when my mum hadn't waited up for him. He'd read this as a sign that 'Naebudy gaves a fuck aboot me'—which he'd cry as the hinge of the oven door screeched open. We'd hear my mum's slippered feet on the landing and her voice of weary acceptance sighing 'Ar shull 'adda goo an' ged 'im ait the oven.'

'Leave him,' we'd shout, and I don't know about my siblings but I for one really meant it.

I despised him and fondly imagined the wonderful and carefree life my mum and I could have without him. Once we actually planned to murder him. My mum said we could take him on a day trip to Beachy Head and lure him to the edge on some pretext then push him off. I really believed that we were going to do this.

Possibly, because of Dad's increasingly repellent behaviour, Chris got married when she was just nineteen. No doubt Dad gobbing Woodbine phlegm up her legs was a driving force, but certainly she felt herself a slightly better class of person than the rest of our family. She had gotten into a catholic girls' grammar school and quickly taken on airs and graces—liking classical music for example. My mum was terribly wounded by her when she found a diary that Chris kept where she'd confided her horror at the thought of Mum going to parents' evening in her yellow mackintosh and green shoes. She expressed similar repulsion at Mum's farting.

***Deborah** wearing her 'not a bridesmaid' dress on Margate beach*

When Chris left her 'beloved' Notre Dame School she worked at Barclays bank, which in our street was a very nice class of job indeed. She married a man called Ken, who had his own plastering business, and prospects. I wasn't allowed to be bridesmaid because, at four, I was still prone to running to my mum and could not be trusted to walk sensibly down the aisle without misadventure. I bore this judgement without complaint because I preferred the orange dress I was bought as a consolation to the horrid creations worn by the official bridesmaids.

As it turned out I had an absolute ball at the wedding. I'd recently perfected the art of doing the 'twist' and spent much of the evening showing off my talents on the stage. My performance won me the attention of a huge number of young women with enormous beehives who worked with my sister at the bank, and in whom I seemed to have aroused incipient maternal feelings. Get it any way you can has always been my motto and I basked in their attentions.

***Deborah** doing the twist at Chris and Ken's wedding (oddly superimposed)*

Meanwhile, the two matriarchs on our side of the family, Scotch Gran and Nan Munroe, had rekindled their friendship over a bottle of 120 proof Whisky and were found outside on the steps steaming drunk, howling with laughter and singing 'I belang tae Glasgow' at the top of their lungs. They had to be carried home. My dad nearly 'put the heed oan' a drunken reveller who staggered dangerously close to me on the stage, nearly knocking me over, but was restrained by a group of the groom's friends. Martin got drunk for the first time on a looted bottle of cider, and was sick. It was an all-round excellent night's entertainment.

A Ghost Boy

Every Friday night after Chris got married Mum, Martin and I went to visit her and Ken at their new 'private' house. They were the first people in our family to own their own home and the first to go on a package holiday to Spain. The working classes were starting to 'make good'. We watched telly and had fish and chips for supper, and sometimes my cousin came round too. I always liked that because she was glamorous and had dated a bloke who played for the Cobblers. This made her almost famous.

One Friday, Martin arrived late. He'd been on a school trip to London Zoo and he said something had bitten him. It wasn't serious, just a nick but he felt tired, so we went home early. Next morning he said he'd got a sore throat and that his back hurt. Mum turned him over in bed and found his back covered in huge open sores. She panicked and sent for an ambulance.

'You coulda got a Winston Churchill five shillin' piece inta the 'oles in his poor little back,' she sobbed to the neighbour.

Martin was whisked into hospital and by the end of the day had symptoms similar to pneumonia, but not pneumonia. As the days passed, Martin's condition deteriorated and the illness from which he suffered could not be diagnosed. By the next Friday night, the doctors told my parents that he would not survive the weekend. He was 11 years old. Mum was completely inconsolable.

Martin did, though, survive the weekend, and in a last-ditch attempt to diagnose his disease a specialist from Oxford was called in. Martin, it seemed, was suffering from a severe form of a rare skin disease called Stevens-Johnson Syndrome. They did not understand at the time how the disease was contracted but the bite at London zoo was thought to be the cause.

This was early July and the annual trip to Margate had to be cancelled as Martin slowly returned to health. That summer my mum spent most of the time going backwards and forwards to the hospital. I wasn't allowed into the buildings for fear of infection and I spent the summer playing in the extensive, wooded hospital grounds. There I met a boy a few years older than me and we got along famously. He was a patient at the hospital but of the non-infectious variety. He was easy to bully and seemed not to mind playing all the games I wanted to play. I thought it grand that a big boy wanted me for a mate, though some days he was pale and too out of sorts to withstand my rough-housing.

On the day my brother was to be discharged, at the beginning of September, I went to find my chum to say goodbye and have one last game of hide and seek. He was nowhere to be found so I petitioned my mum to help me. We went to the boys' ward, and there a nurse whispered to my mum that he'd been terminally ill and had died the previous evening. I felt a terrible eeriness and sense of loss that I was unable to articulate. I've always felt as though I spent that strange summer playing with a ghost child, the ghost my brother nearly was. It was as if the breath of mortality had whistled through our family but settled in another.

The postponed holiday to Margate was resurrected and arrangements were made for Mum, Martin and me to go in the second week of September as part of Martin's convalescence. Martin was still incredibly frail and my mum was fraught from the stress of nearly losing him. I didn't get much of a look in, in terms of attention, and the bitter-cold autumn sea breeze nearly froze our bones. So, in spite of getting away from Dad for a week, the holiday was a disappointment and we were glad when the Saturday arrived and he came with his mate, who owned a Zephyr, to pick us up.

Martin's *convalescent holiday - Margate 1963*

While we'd been away though, there'd been trouble at home. On the Tuesday night, Dad had been to the pub and got home to find Gerry having a coffee with her boyfriend, Cliff, at the kitchen table. Dad went to bed and Gerry saw Cliff out and went to bed herself. The older Jerry though had not, gone peacefully to sleep but had lain awake, seething with who-knows-what in his unhinged mind.

In the middle of the night Gerry was abruptly woken as the lights were switched on in her bedroom and a large suitcase landed on her as she lay in bed. Dad's eyes were on fire with menace and he grabbed her and dragged her out of bed screaming 'Get the fuck oot o' thus hoose.'

She didn't argue, just threw on a coat and ran into the night. She met a policeman at the top of the street and he escorted her to her friend's house where she spent the rest of that week.

When my mum found out she went mad and, as usual when he'd done something heinous, Dad was contrite. Gerry was reinstated in the household, but the incident revealed my dad's dark and disturbed thoughts and his precarious ability to control them.

Gerry (I)

While Chris went to Notre Dame School, Gerry failed her Eleven Plus exam and went to the worst secondary modern in Northampton, Spencer Girls School, where she spent four years at the back of the class making monkey noises. She left at fifteen and got a job as a machinist at 'The Brook', an underwear manufacturer. She hung out with a crowd of unruly young women who I thought fabulous. They wore beehives, mascara that you spat in and pan-stick foundation. One of them, Marilyn, could light matches off the seat of her mini skirt. Sometimes they took me on Saturday afternoons to an underground café where I drank Pepsi Cola and played Beatles songs on the jukebox. This to me was the very height of bliss.

Gerry smoked N°6 cigarettes, drank vodka and lime and went to low dives and notorious pubs. At one of these she met her future husband, Cliff Ward, or Scottie as he was known about town. He was, like our dad, a Scot. He was also a violent petty criminal and a chronic fantasist. He imagined himself a big-time player with a fabulous life of wealth and riches. In reality his criminal exploits never went beyond robbing fags from the corner shop and selling 'bathtub blues'. But he was charming and generous with a sense of *joie de vie* that made him shine in the drab drear of the working-class Northampton 1960s. I could see why Gerry loved him, even if no one else could. Mum and Dad though measured Gerry's boyfriends against the virtues of Chris's husband Ken and found them wanting, particularly in the case of Cliff, who clearly was a wrong-un. But nothing they could say or do would put her off him. She loved him and stayed loyal to him in the face of all their criticism.

One cold winter Friday night Gerry went out on a date with Cliff with strict instructions to be back by 11pm. She had the only house key. I don't know why we only had one key but it was 1963 and keys didn't grow on trees. Mum, Martin and me had been on our weekly visit to Chris and Ken and got home just after eleven to find ourselves locked out. A tense wait followed. Mum was terrified of the fearful row that would erupt if Gerry didn't arrive home before Dad. I stood sentry, swinging on the front gate. To my horror it was Dad that rounded the corner and came down the street swaying slightly from drink. He was in a nasty mood. 'Ull hov t'break the fuckin' windae,' he roared.

Mum begged him to wait a few minutes, knowing that Gerry would be on the last bus. He ignored her and, in his alcohol-induced rage, took a spade out of the shed.

'Don't, Dad, please, she'll be home in a minute,' Martin implored him, as Jerry swung the tool with all his force at the side window. It had eight small frames and every one of them shattered, spraying a constellation of glass across the living-room floor. The window, once opened, proved too small for an adult to pass through, so Dad told Martin to climb in and come round to the kitchen door to let us in. My mum sobbed and begged some more,

'He'll cut hisself Jerry. Please don't make him. 'E's ony jus' come ait the bloody hospital.'

Dad shrugged her off. 'Och awae we ye, ye dozy arsed woman.'

Martin climbed through, snagging his jacket on shards of jagged glass sticking out of the ruined window. He tumbled slightly as he clambered into the room and cut his knee on one of the million tiny fragments glinting in the carpet. Just as he unlocked the back door, Gerry came down the entry, the worse for Vodka. Her mascara was smudged inkily down her face and the backcombing was coming out of her beehive.

'Wit time d'ye call this? An' look at the fuckin' state o'ye,' Dad bellowed at her. 'Hov ye been wi' that fuckin' Cliff Ward again?'

He staggered dangerously towards her. Mum tried to intervene saying, 'You goo up t'bed Gerry. Let me sort it all out.'

We all hovered around on the stairs but no one dared go to bed. The row raged on, and as usual ended with him accusing everyone of hating him and threatening to kill us all and himself. Then he picked up a razor blade and cut his wrist. Gerry ran out of the house and up the street to fetch a policeman. I've always thought her terribly brave for this action. Either the bloodletting or the prospect of the police coming to the house seemed to calm him down. When Gerry got back to the house with a policeman in tow, Dad stood, hands behind his back, and explained it had all been a 'misunderstanding'.

'Just a wee bit o' a family barny, mate. Nothing t' worry aboot.'

'Have you cut yourself, Jock? Do you want to let me have a look at it?'

'Och it's a wee scratch from breaking the windae t'get intae the hoose.'

'Oh well then, if you're sure, Jock, I'll leave you all in peace.' The policeman was more than happy not to get involved in a 'domestic'.

I was hiding underneath the kitchen table watching drops of blood from his wrist plop onto the lino.

Gerry interceded. 'What d'you think he's gunna do when you've gone and we're on ere own with him again?'

'There's nothing to be done here, love. Your dad's fine now and I'm only up the street if there's any more bother.' And with that the policeman left. Mum made a cup of tea and the calm held that night. The next morning Dad was overbearingly matey with us all, especially Gerry. She'd shown him that she could stand up to him and she'd shown me, through her actions, that our dad's behaviour was a long way from normal.

During Gerry and Cliff's courtship we had a peeping tom. The neighbours from across the back gardens had spotted a man prowling around by our sheds. Gerry and Cliff had suspected as much when their passion had been interrupted by occasional crashing in the garden. An ambush was planned for the next night. The neighbours would signal by switching their lights on and off twice. Gerry and Cliff took up their 'snogging on the settee' position, except this time Cliff slid a carving knife down the side of the chair. My dad was stationed upstairs armed with a pair of dress-making scissors. This was all terrific fun for me. We hadn't got a telly in those days so it broke the monotony. Mum and Gerry were scared of what might happen if they caught him. It hadn't really occurred to me that they would actually use these gruesome weapons on another human being. When the lights flashed on and off Dad and Cliff raced outside, but the peeping Tom had seen the signal too, and with fantastic athleticism ran off, hurdling the fences as he went. They didn't catch him. They did though get close enough to identify him as the simple-minded son of our next door neighbour, who had long had a crush on Gerry. He never peeped in our windows again but, Mum shrewdly observed, 'She must've bin giving 'im summat to bloody well look at.'

We had dinner at dinner time in those days; 12 o'clock. Martin and I came home from school. Dad and Gerry came home from their respective factories, and Chris, though already married, came from the bank. We always had the same thing on the same day of the week, so I know this was a Thursday because we were having meat pie and gravy made with the leftovers of Wednesday's stew. As Mum was clearing away the plates, Gerry asked her for a private talk. They went into hall, and after 5 minutes of muffled mumbling we heard Gerry put her coat on and go out. Mum came back into the kitchen.

'Well, she's got herself up the stick,' she said ruefully. 'She's in the family way.'

At this, Chris stood up and ran sobbing out of the room. With all the drama it seemed inappropriate to ask for bananas and custard. When Chris had composed herself, she came back into the kitchen.

'I wanted to be the first to give you a grandchild,' she sniffled into her hanky. 'Trust her to beat me. She's as common as muck, not even engaged.' Angry, she tucked the hanky back up her sleeve.

'Aye, wull see aboot that,' Dad said, rage barely suppressed.

A marriage was speedily arranged. As it happened though, Gerry had a miscarriage a week before the wedding. Mum pleaded with her not to marry him. She said it wasn't too late to call the whole thing off. Gerry wouldn't listen. She said she loved him and would marry him anyway so why not straight away. And marry him she did, the next

Saturday in a navy-blue shift-dress. After the wedding party they went to the room with a kitchenette they had rented in a lodging house. The next morning the young couple were awoken early by Cliff's dad hammering on the front door. He'd come to see if there was any booze left over from the party.

***Gerry** (with beehive), **Chris** and **Deborah**(with chocolate-finger ciggie) - Chris' house, Christmas 1968*

Guess Who's Dead

Dorothy continued her affair with Bert throughout the early 1960s. Bert worked for the Ministry of Agriculture. I'm not sure exactly what he did, but once he confided in Dorothy about an incident at work that had troubled his conscience. Part of his role was administering poisons and a farmer had asked him for a quantity of arsenic for the purpose of killing vermin. Bert knew the man's wife had just died and that he really wanted the poison to commit suicide. He gave him the arsenic and the man did kill himself. He'd asked Dorothy if this made him a murderer. I don't know how she dealt with this philosophical problem but she discussed it with me and it was my first realisation that academic questions of morality existed. Nobody in my universe had ever given me any indication that human thought processes went far beyond food and sex. Bert was deeper and more mysterious than anybody I'd ever come into contact with.

He called at our house frequently during the day when Dad was at work. Sometimes he walked from the government buildings and sometimes he arrived in a posh car. I know this because I was regularly off school. I loathed and dreaded school because it meant being away from my mum and that filled me with fear and loneliness. Sometimes I feigned illness and sometimes Mum just let me stay off because she liked the company. When Bert arrived I was sent into the garden to play. Once I ran into the kitchen and Bert was standing in front of my mum as she hurriedly did up her zip-front dress. When Bert left I told her what I'd seen. She laughed and did a saucy whistle that made me laugh too. After that when she whistled and mimed doing up her zip it was a secret code reminding me of the confidences we shared.

One Monday morning Mum said I could stay off school because Bert was coming to see us. He'd been on holiday in Tel Aviv and had sent a postcard saying: See you Monday morning for coffee. Have gifts for you and Deborah. Ever, Bert.

Mum had the kettle boiling ready at eleven but Bert didn't show up. She waited in increasing annoyance until we had to go out to visit Chris as Mum always did on a

Monday afternoon. When we got there Chris had a copy of Saturday's 'Chronicle and Echo' in front of her,

'Guess who's dead?' she quizzed Mum glibly.

'Who?' Mum said.

'That Bert Hendry who you know,' Chris nonchalantly replied. 'He's had a massive heart attack in Tel Aviv.'

'Oh.' Mum's voice only just maintained equilibrium. She took up the newspaper and pretended to read as she choked back the tears that flooded her eyes.

Chris was busy putting the kettle on and didn't notice Mum's reaction. To Chris, Bert was a casual acquaintance. She had no idea of the length and the depth of Mum's relationship which had lasted over a decade by this time.

We stayed for as long as Mum could stand it. I never took my eyes off her in case she should break down or falter. She didn't in front of Chris, whose attitudes and values allowed for no indiscretions or acts of commonness. When we left the tears flowed, and by the time we were on the number seventeen bus she was sobbing uncontrollably. I did my best to soothe her agitation, but at eight years old I was ill-equipped to deal with grief of this magnitude. When we got home she went to her bedroom where I could hear her sobs interspersed with screaming. I sat downstairs in the chilly twilight, dreading Dad coming home to find his tea unmade and his wife destroyed by the loss of her lover. When he did, he went upstairs, blacked her eye, and then went out for fish and chips.

Horror Stories

In today's world of diagnosis and labelling I would be school-phobic, which is odd, given that I've been a teacher for the last seventeen years. I hated and feared school as a kid, and my mum conspired with me in staying away as often as I could. I wasn't really bullied any more than the next person. I did get upset when a kid kept kneeing me up the bum when we were lining up to go in and some wag used to take a bite out of the finger of fudge I always had in my satchel. This impertinence progressed until they'd eaten the whole thing and left me the wrapper, but it wasn't exactly the stuff of nightmares.

I'd do anything to stay at home with my mum. Amateur psychoanalysts will probably posit that I feared my mum would go away as soon as my back was turned. In fact, my mum was just a whole lot more entertaining than Janet and John books and the enforced consumption of warm school milk.

As I set out to school one day I saw a kid called Horace Story who lived in our street. He was a simple, spotty, bespectacled, gangling boy known locally as 'Horror Story'. 'Horror' was about fourteen. I must have been seven and I decided to go home and tell Mum he'd hit me so I wouldn't have to go to school. It worked, but Mum was livid and said 'Om not 'avin it. Om gooin' up that bloody school an' tellin' the headmaster.'

I was horrified that my little ruse was going to be busted and did everything I could to dissuade her from this course of action, even offering to go to school, but she was adamant. We marched up to Spencer Boys School. I was rehearsing telling her the truth in my head but the words grouped then dissipated, unspoken, in my mouth. When we arrived we were shown into the head's office. On hearing my mum's account of this fictitious beating, he sent at once for the alleged perpetrator. This was it. I would be shown up for the lying little toe-rag that I was.

The poor shabby fellow arrived at the head's office in his horn-rimmed national health glasses and looked forlornly from me to my mum. The head presented him with my accusation and, to my utter amazement, he admitted to the crime. He was forced to make a humble apology to me and the head assured my mum he'd have six of the best after we'd gone. I got a Caramac on the way home and my mum was satisfied that justice had been served. This incident did me no good at all. The guilt I felt was totally corrosive. Weirdly, every time Horace saw me after that he smiled and I looked quickly away. Maybe he wasn't such a simpleton after all.

I couldn't read or write before I went to school and I remember on my first day feeling ashamed when we were asked to write our names. I went home for dinner and angrily entreated my mum to teach me how to write 'Debbie Gibbons'. She did, and I found that the letters came easily, but no one had thought to show me this skill before. There were no children's books in our house, other than my brother's 'Guinness Book of Records', so literacy wasn't high on my agenda—although I could have told you the weight of the fattest man in the world and how long the longest cucumber. Dad stopped reading after the telly came in and Mum read true murder. So although she didn't read to me as such, she did tell me tales of Jack the Ripper, Crippen, Christie and Haigh. My mum could tell a great story and I was well versed in nineteenth and twentieth century horrors before I went to school.

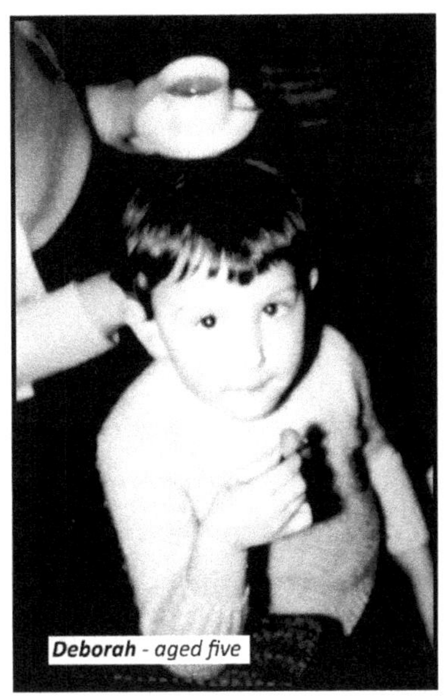
Deborah - *aged five*

Her particular favourite was Alfred Arthur Rouse, because this notorious murder had actually happened in Northampton when she was a girl of ten. Rouse 'travelled in ladies underwear'. People did in those days. He was a philanderer and petty criminal who had managed to get himself into a mess of debt and pregnant women. He needed to die and start again, so he befriended a friendless itinerant and over a period of months established that this man was alone in the world. On Guy Fawkes' Night 1931, he drove the man to a lonely lane in Hardingstone, at that time a village on the outskirts of Northampton. He stalled his vehicle and got out pretending to his new 'friend' that he was tinkering with the engine. Instead he took a wrench from the boot and smashed the tramp's head in with it. He then put the body into the driver's seat and marked it with distinguishing items: his wedding ring, watch etc. When he was satisfied that the tramp would be assigned the wrong identity he set the car alight. If seen, it would be regarded as just another bonfire. Rouse made his escape across the fields towards Northampton town. The perfect murder? No, as it turned out, because two revellers returning from a party saw Rouse running, lit by his own fire as he fled across Delapre Abbey. My mum actually knew one of these men. He was called Ginger Munns and he alerted the Police.

Rouse was arrested and tried for murder at Northampton assizes the following March. During the trial Rouse's loyal wife stayed in Northampton and got a temporary job in a sweet shop in the town centre. That sweet shop did a roaring trade. My mum went in for a quarter of buttered Brazils every day.

The trial also attracted the attention of the media, and the socialite and journalist Sybil Cookson covered it for one of the weekly journals. Sybil Cookson was at the time the lover of the famous, but now virtually lost and unacknowledged lesbian artist 'Gluck', who did two studies of the trial: 'The Expert Witness' and 'The Unofficial Jury'. Gluck's work is an invaluable part of lesbian history. The iconic 'YouWe' (used as the cover of the Virago edition of 'The Well of Loneliness' showing her and the love of her life, Nesta Obermer, in profile) is possibly the most powerful lesbian image ever made. It is owned by the National Gallery and lies mouldering in a storage unit in Merton, an indictment of the invisibility of lesbians even in this supposedly enlightened twenty-first century.

Rouse was convicted and sentenced to hang. As he walked, condemned, from the court he turned to the public and ran his hand across his throat. The tramp lies buried in Hardingstone churchyard. A simple wooden cross marks the spot: The Grave of an Unknown Man.

Murder yarns were my absolute favourite. Mum and I spent hours discussing the possible Ripper suspects. Mum's preference was the 'Jill the Ripper' theory, though I always favoured the idea of the vengeful, bereaved surgeon, whose son had died from a dose of the pox acquired after an encounter with a prostitute. Understandably, Dorothy had a strong sense of empathy with the luckless victims of these crimes.

The process of justice in England is littered with miscarriages, and these were a source of outrage to us both—none more so than the case of Edith Thompson. It was easy to see how women across the country identified with this flighty, romantic young woman trapped in an arid loveless marriage. Thompson had fallen for a tempestuous young sailor boy, Frederick Bywaters. One night he got drunk and waited in the shadows for his lover and her husband to return from a night out. In the scuffle that ensued, Bywaters fatally stabbed Percy Thompson. The lovers were both put on trial for murder, though witnesses made it quite clear that Edith Thompson had been as surprised as her husband by the attack.

During the trial compromising letters detailing her hatred for her husband and her sexual infidelity with Bywaters, whom she saw as her 'true' husband, were read out in court. An all-male jury delivered a verdict of guilty and Thompson and Bywaters were sentenced to hang. F. Tennyson Jesse was a journalist who covered the trial and afterwards wrote her fictionalised account 'A Pin to see the Peep Show', which in my view is the greatest polemic against capital punishment ever written. Even Virginia Woolf noted the travesty of justice in her diary. In a complicated and strange entry Woolf wrote of hearing a woman cry out in the street at night 'as if in anguish'. It was 7th January 1923, two days before the execution and she wrote: I thought of Mrs Thompson waiting to be hanged.

When Mum went to see Bonnie and Clyde at the pictures in 1967 she came to my bedroom that night to tell me all about it and cursed the X certificate that prevented me from seeing it too. Bonnie Parker was another romantic young woman caught up in a tragic *folie a deux* with the brutalised petty criminal, Clyde Barrow. After a life of grinding poverty in the American dust bowl of the 1930s, the pair went on a lunatic bank-robbing spree. They were shot to death in Technicolor slow motion. Their bodies riddled with one hundred and sixty-eight bullets in a terrible St Vitas dance of death.

'Ooh, ere Deb, you shoulda seen it,' Mum lamented.

I was twelve when the film '10 Rillington Place' came out and I was desperate to go with Mum and Gerry to the Odeon to see it. They dressed and made me up to look older, even giving me one of Gerry's fags to hold in the queue as a prop. It worked and I sneaked past the usherette unchallenged.

The film dramatised the case of John Christie. It was one that had exercised me and Mum for years. Not only was it a monstrous tale of patriarchal serial killing and necrophilia, but also a notorious miscarriage of justice. Christie murdered desperate young women seeking illegal abortions during the London blitz. After he'd murdered his victims, he walled their bodies up in his house keeping grotesque trophies of their pubic hair for his later delectation. Two of his victims were the wife and young child of his lodger, Timothy Evans. This twenty-five year-old man with an IQ of seventy was wrongly arrested and convicted of their murders. He hanged in 1950. Christie confessed to these and the other killings three years later.

It may not have been a diet of fairy tales but it was a stimulating and thought provoking education. In the strobe-light scrutiny of modern thought on child development, my experiences would today be considered damaging, even abusive. This is not the case as I see it. My mum may have lacked appropriate boundaries when it came to her sex life, she may have discussed events and issues outside the normal experience of a young child, but she showered me with love. I never doubted once that I was adored by her. And in loving her in response I had the best training in how to love another person anyone could ever wish for.

Though I was late with literacy I was well advanced in arithmetic. My family liked to play cards and Dad taught me complex games. From the age of four I could play grown-up games requiring skill, like Brag and Napoleon. I recall one Saturday night, after my mum and dad had got home from the pub, being woken up by Dad and made to come downstairs and play Brag with a black man who they'd bought back to the house for 'coffee'. I was five. Ok, this might be veering close to abusive, given that, almost certainly, the man was some type of punter. I played a number of hands of Nine-card Brag with the man and won the ten shilling wager, which I was allowed to keep. No doubt this was some demonstration of the superiority of the white races on the part of my dad. I will leave the psychoanalysis to those better qualified than me.

Dad's Accident

Dad rode a motorbike. It was a Francis Barnett 250. He went to work on it every day. We all wondered if he ever had fits on his bike. It seemed highly likely that he did. By this time, 1967, he was having several each day and still refusing to seek medical advice. No one dared argue with him about it, since not only would this have been to acknowledge his epilepsy but he was also drinking heavily and his behaviour was increasingly erratic and violent.

A law making crash helmets compulsory was to come in the following January and Chris had bought Dad his first helmet for his birthday on the 13th of November. That was a Monday. On the Friday, just as Mum and I were making ham sandwiches for tea, a loud knock came to the door. I answered,

'Mum, it's a copper,' I shouted back into the kitchen.

Mum came racing out in a screaming panic crying 'Oh no not my boy. Please God not my Martin.'

'No love, it's your husband. He's had an accident.'

'Thank God,' Mum answered the startled officer.

We went to the hospital in the police car. Dad had a broken femur and severe concussion. His new crash helmet had a massive dent in it and the doctor explained to us how he'd have been dead without it. Mum and I looked ruefully at each other. He'd hit a lorry, somersaulted into the air and landed on his head. The doctor also asked Mum what she knew about the epileptic fits. His illness was, at long last, diagnosed. For the rest of his life he took a high dose of Phenobarbitone. They explained to Mum that had he not been diagnosed he would have been dead in six months anyway. So the accident had saved his life.

The good news was that he'd be in hospital for the next three months. We went home on the bus, threw the clothes they'd cut off him on some waste-ground and went to the chip shop for supper to celebrate. I slept in my mum's bed that whole freezing winter.

While Dad was in hospital money was even more tight than usual. Mum was still seeing Martin's real dad, George, and he helped out a lot. I knew all about the relationship but Martin still had no clue. Mum protected him and feared he'd be disgusted and stop loving her if he found out.

One night, Mum was entertaining George downstairs and I'd been sent to bed early with a comic and a bag of crisps. As I lay reading the Beano I heard Martin's Lambretta scooter pull up outside unexpectedly. He was supposed to be at his girlfriend's house that night. There was nothing I could do to warn Mum. I heard Martin walk into the house and open the living-room door. Mum and George were having sex on the floor. Martin silently turned around and walked out of the house. I heard his scooter start and he rode away. Here was another event when I was called upon to deal with Mum's torment. Of course, this was beyond my capabilities.

Martin never mentioned the incident. He stopped speaking to Mum for about a fortnight and he had a recurrence of his illness, as he tended in times of stress. Mum fretted and worried and cooked all his favourite dinners. The event stayed unmentioned until recently when I told Martin that George was his real dad and we talked about what happened. I'd wanted to tell him for years but I think I'd picked up Mum's habit of protecting him from things that might hurt him. After he got used to the idea I think he was glad that our 'Dad' wasn't actually his dad and who could blame him.

After Dad came out of hospital his mad drinking behaviour continued, and this was now compounded by the strong barbiturate he'd been prescribed. In fact, these new pills replaced the oven as a prop in the suicide game he played. At times he'd come in staggering drunk and wake Martin and try to fight him. Maybe he knew that Martin wasn't his son, but personally, I don't think so. I think it was some kind of assertion of his masculinity and his general distrust of Martin's gentle, pacific nature. You can take the boy out of the Gorbals but you can't take the Gorbals out of the boy. He was out of place and out of time. When Martin did not respond he'd pick a fight with Mum or accuse me of looking at him with sheer hatred. He wasn't wrong there. When these attempts at coercion failed he'd take all his Phenobarbitone tablets. On those occasions Mum stayed up all night making sure he vomited rather than letting him go to sleep and choke to death. More than any other time, in those dark days I wished him dead.

Grammar School

In spite of my terrible attendance record I did pass my Eleven Plus exam. We'd moved, when I was nine, to yet another horrible, scruffy council house, but one that bordered a posher area. As a result I went to a new primary school, and in so doing massively improved my chances of passing this notoriously culturally 'middle class' exam. On my first day at the new school I was sat on a table with a group of very able middle class and upper working class girls. Their dads were foremen in factories or even accountants, and some of them had Mums who went out to work in offices. They lived in centrally heated houses with fitted carpets and cultivated gardens. We'd always had a garden but Dad thought that men who did their gardens were queers who hated their wives. So our garden was an overgrown forest of weeds and constant source of argument.

These able girls were an inspiration to me and I raised my game at school to fit in. We were the favoured group. Our teacher, a Miss Voss, doted on us all. She would go round our table and, leaning over me to correct my grammar, rest one enormous bosom heavily on my shoulder. There's something strangely comforting about a huge breast on your shoulder and I liked school a little better.

Things got serious, though, in the last year of primary school. We were split into a top class of thirty who were to be trained to pass the exam by Mr York, and four classes of others who were entered for the exam but given no preparation. I got into the top class, mostly by the fluke of having this new group of pals.

Mr York was a scary figure. No doubt a quite brilliant pedagogue but very strict and driven in his quest to get us all through the exam. On our first week in his class we were put into seats in alphabetical order and told on no account were we to be allowed to go to the toilet or leave the room for any other reason and presented with a 'mock' exam. It was a series of anagrams and codes. I had never seen such a thing before and had absolutely no idea what to do. I pissed myself. At ten years old this was ignominy beyond endurance. When the papers were collected in, Mr York looked down at the floor beneath my seat and told me to wait outside. Then he took me home in his car. He put a newspaper on the seat for me to sit on. He asked my mum if I had 'problems' and said that though I stood no chance of passing my exams he would allow me stay in the top class.

Every week that year we were given mock exams and by Christmas I'd learned the tricks and code-breakers I needed. When we did the exams in May I knew for certain that I had 100% on my mathematics paper. I'd completed it within half the time and had time to check and double check every question. I passed with flying-colours and opted with my mates to go to Trinity, the only co-educational grammar school in town.

Social class was still, in the 1960's, an issue. It meant something to be working class. Now there is only wealth and poverty. The working class and middle class merged in Thatcher's Britain of the 1980's. Workers bought their council houses and shares in the formerly nationally owned utilities companies, thus depriving their own children of the right to decent housing and shared wealth. How prophetic was Karl Marx? The false consciousness of greed and acquisition consumed the nation. Working class culture sank into something sociologists identified as the underclass. A kind of criminal sub-culture exemplified today by the 'hilarious' exploits of the Gallagher family in 'Shameless'. What an appropriate title for a programme devoted to the ridicule of the poor and the mentally ill.

On my first day at grammar school it was apparent that I was working class. My jumper was just the wrong shade of green and went bobbly by Christmas. In a school of eight hundred kids, I'd say about ten were working class. One fifth of the school's intake were girls, who had to achieve a higher grade than boys to pass the Eleven Plus exam. The wisdom being that girls would not need qualifications since they were to be housewives and mothers, and boys mature later so they would overtake their female peers during the course of secondary school. Oh, that's all right then!

The whole ludicrous exam was of course an IQ test, predicated on the work and research of the educational psychologist Cyril Burt. Burt believed intelligence to be genetically inherited and tested his theory on monozygotic twins separated at birth. When the tripartite education system was introduced in 1944, working class kids were to be given the opportunity to go to grammar school by passing the exam. The vast majority didn't, because the questions were culturally specific—unscrambling anagrams of the names of the classical composers for example. Bourdieu was yet to name 'cultural capital' but working class and black kids failed these tests in vast numbers. Burt's work was discredited in 1976, when it was discovered that the researchers who had supposedly tested the fifty-five sets of monozygotic, separated twins had never actually existed. It seems highly unlikely that Burt had somehow got hold of fifty-five sets of these twins who had been conveniently separated in any case. The fact that a couple of generations of British youngsters had their lives determined by this fraudster has pretty much gone un-remarked.

My mum was shoplifting by the time I went to grammar school. I was often with her on these hair-raising sprees. In fact I stole the white, leather-bound prayer book that was part of the endless 'uniform list' we'd been sent in the summer before I started. We thought that a pair of compasses meant that you needed two of them, yet annoyingly there was only one in the geometry set Mum nicked from Marks the Stationer and we had to buy another one.

When I was twelve, the terrible thing happened. Mum got caught. I was with her when a middle-aged woman with an apoplectic face and no compassion slapped a fat hand on my mum's shoulder and asked us to accompany her to the manager's office. She'd stolen a set of cutlery and other kitchen equipment to help Gerry get set up in her new house. Mum pleaded my innocence with them and begged them to let me go. They didn't believe her. We were taken to the police station and finger-printed. They kept us there all Saturday afternoon. At about six o'clock, Dad arrived to fetch us. He was annoyed with her for getting caught. Mum was charged and released on bail. They didn't charge me.

The case came up three months later. Mum got fined £40, which she borrowed from Martin, who was by this time working. The real punishment was the piece that appeared in the local paper, quite a big article on page three with a fair-sized headline. There'd be no way any of my schoolmates or teachers would miss it. No one ever mentioned it, but I could see in their eyes that they'd seen it. I lived for years with a terrible sense of mortification.

I didn't do well at Trinity. Not only did I have serious social-class inferiority but I'd also begun to realise that liking girls in a romantic way was not what was supposed to happen.

I Was a Teenage Lesbian

Don't be fooled by the porno title, this was no fun. It felt fabulous in my heart to love other girls, a wonderful, precious secret. But the outside world must never know. Homosexuality had been decriminalized in 1967 but attitudes had not shifted an inch by the early 1970s. At least they hadn't in Northampton.

My sexual orientation has nothing to do with sex and genitalia. I loved women and wanted to be near them and talk to them and be loved by them. I have never been able to love a man in the same way. When I was a teenager this was categorized as a mental illness. It was 1976 before homosexuality was removed from the Diagnostic and Statistical Manual of Mental Illnesses.

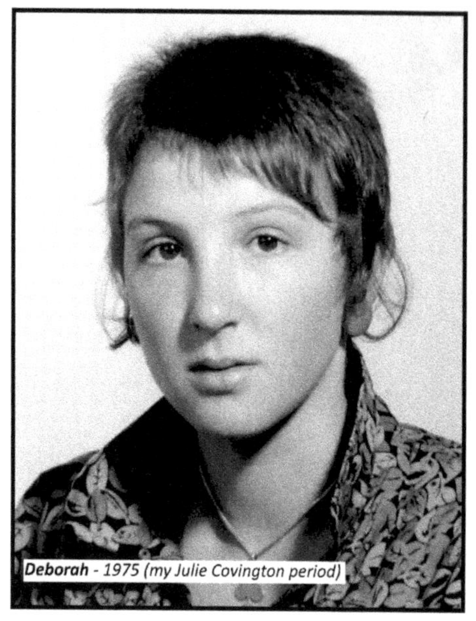
Deborah - 1975 (my Julie Covington period)

I was the first among my circle of friends to get a boyfriend and the first to have sex. Neither of these acts was sensibly thought through as a plan of action to 'prove' my heterosexuality. Everything I did was an emotional train crash—a horrible M25 pile up of neediness, confusion, fear and destruction. I eventually walked away from the smouldering wreckage, but there were some casualties on the way.

At fourteen I started going out with a boy who, foolishly, I later married. He wore makeup, a long leather coat and platform shoes. He worshipped Mick Jagger and then he worshipped me. He was one of eleven children and his house was much scruffier than mine, so I never felt embarrassed about him coming there.

After we'd been seeing each other for a while our snogging turned to petting, and he asked me to have intercourse with him. I agreed—through wanting to get it over with rather than anything even vaguely resembling desire. We arranged to meet at his sister's flat where we did most of our courting. It was a filthy ground-floor in an old Victorian house. His sister, Jackie, was in her twenties and had a child and a junkie husband. She herself practiced witchcraft under the tutelage of her much older lover, a crag-faced warlock of indeterminate middle age.

We did it in Jackie's bed, where there was every indication that she had recently entertained both the junkie and the warlock. It was an inauspicious place to lose your virginity. I found it excruciatingly painful. But my physical discomfort paled into insignificance when I realized that two of my boyfriend's mates were outside the bedroom window peering in. He'd obviously been boasting to them and they'd decided to check it out themselves. That night I wheeled my bike home with a feeling of damp soreness at the heart of me.

I never told my friends at school, though of course, information like this soon emanates around such a small community. I felt different to my friends both in terms of class and sexuality. I knew beyond a shadow of a doubt that I would never be part of a world of sensible bedtimes, revision schedules and home improvements. Some of my friends had parents who were teachers and even university lecturers. This was utterly alienating to me. Being around people who seemed so secure with their place in the world pushed me further to the margins.

My very best friend, Sue, was a little closer to me in terms of class—at least her dad worked in a factory. He was, though, a foreman in an engineering firm and he was the most learned adult I knew. He once described to me how he had cried when at the end of the TV series 'The Ascent of Man' Jacob Bronowski had picked up a handful of soil from Auschwitz and adjured the audience that such a thing must never happen again. Hearing an adult talk with so much passion and intellect was at the same time wonderful and crushing because it made my situation seem infinitely worse. With middle-class people, there is a reserve, an unbridgeable distance. I wanted to be with them and I lied to make myself fit but I also needed the solace of those who not only knew material poverty but who shared my cultural background. So I carried on seeing the ungallant boyfriend, and I hung out with gangs of kids without aspiration who didn't care that my mum was a shoplifter.

It was around this time Mum told me that Bert was in all likelihood my real father. This was a happy turn of events because it freed me from any biological connection to Jerry Gibbons. It also meant that there was a strong possibility that all four of us siblings had different fathers. Way to go, Mum!

This mattered not one bit to me. Everything is about with whom you've shared a life. So although Jerry Gibbons wasn't my dad, he was the man whose shadow loomed over my growing up and it was my responses to him that helped form the person I became. I was just happy not to inherit this particular genetic imprint. I remembered Bert with his foreign manners and his secret life and I was glad he was my father. I was to discover much more about him later, but when I was fourteen that was still a long way off.

Mum and I loved walking and during our rambles I'd tell her how I wanted to be a journalist and have a smart flat in London, and that I'd be able to look after her and take her to New York on an aeroplane. I thought all of this was achievable. What I didn't understand was that to her this was a wild fantasy, probably much like the murdering Dad fantasy we'd shared when I was little.

When I asked if I could stay on at school and do 'A' levels with all my mates the answer was an absolute 'No'. We couldn't afford it, and anyway it was a waste to educate a girl who'd marry and never need qualifications. Nothing I could do or say made any difference to their resolve. They needed the money my wages from work would bring to the household.

I did elaborate budget planning showing how they could afford it and how I'd be able to pay them back. I begged. I cried. I said they couldn't stop me, that I didn't need their support. But the truth was I did, and it wasn't there. I had to leave at sixteen and get a job. I was the only one of my mates who did. Everyone else was staying on and planning to go to university. I pretended it was my choice to leave school. I didn't want my middle-class friends to feel sorry for me or think ill of my parents.

I went from one miserable menial job to another. I carried on seeing the boy who would eventually be my husband, but he'd changed from a dangerous, rebel in black mascara into a motorbike salesman in an anorak. I began to despise him and I started experimenting with drugs behind his back.

One of my many tedious jobs was at a jewellery shop in town. Thursday afternoon was early closing in those days and I went to a friend's house, a Jewish boy called Mark. He was radical and hippy and I took my first trip with him. It blew my mind. I have never regretted taking LSD and think it should be available on the National Health. LSD makes a small chemical change in the brain revealing another way of seeing that intensifies and deepens human experience. It was a kind of intellectual and creative booster pill. Like any kind of education, once you've got it no one can ever take it away from you. We listened to 'Wish You Were Here' by Pink Floyd, ate Muesli and painted pictures with our fingers dipped in reds and gold. We tried to make love, but Mark was a sensitive boy and this was enhanced by the drug. He said: 'You're not here, with your mind' and I cried because I knew that I could go on having sex with men but I was never going to be there. He rolled a joint instead and we talked, but I never told him I liked girls. I couldn't because he was in the sixth form at school with my girlfriends and they might think I fancied them if they knew.

This developing awareness of my sexual orientation and the fact that I loathed my mind-numbing job added insult to the injury of being a teenager. I started to see a doctor at the local GP surgery. This had begun with my trying to get sick notes to stay off work and ended with him trying to feel my breast. In between these two events, I'd unwisely trusted him and confided in him about my feelings for girls and my occasional drug use. When I rejected his advance he had me put in the local loony bin, 'St Crispin's'. He wrote a note calling me a deviant Paranoid Schizophrenic to his chum, a psychiatrist, who threatened to have me sectioned if I would not agree to be admitted voluntarily. I spent the bleakest week of my life there and I don't want to revisit this time.

My life lurched from one pitiable event to another. After the horror of a mental institution I needed to get away from my life and from everyone I knew. I was unemployed and found a job working as an au pair for a Swiss family. It was the summer of 1976, the hottest on record. Mum took me to Sywell, a tiny airport near Northampton to meet my new employer. He gave her £100 in cash, a small fortune at the time. She was completely overawed by the wealth and largess of the man. The true motivation for this payment only occurred to me later.

He flew me in a private aircraft to a small airfield somewhere near Zurich, then drove at terrifying speed into the Alps where the family spent the summer. I had to ask him to stop so I could get out and throw up. On the way he kept getting my knee mixed up with the gear stick. I was homesick and scared.

The wife seemed downtrodden by both her husband and her mother. The latter was a housework tyrant who followed me around, showing me how to perform unfathomable tasks, like stoning cherries, and berating me in broken English for having poor window-cleaning skills. There were two children, one of whom had severe learning difficulties.

My job was caring for the children, doing all the housework, acting as sous chef to the wife, waitressing and washing up after every meal. At the end of each day I had to bar my bedroom door against the attentions of the husband. On more than one occasion this involved shouldering my door shut as he tried to barge in. They were super rich and owned not just an aircraft but a yacht.

He took me and the children wind-surfing on Lake Zug where my ability to absorb this new skill was hampered by the huge stiffy he had pressed in the small of my back as he showed me how to master the sail.

On my eighteenth birthday we went to Geneva. I had been led to believe this was some species of birthday treat for me. In fact we visited the husband's sister, a Jackie Kennedy lookalike, who on my arrival showed me to the kitchen and gave me a list, in English, of the tasks I was to perform and instructed me on how to serve at table. I spent the evening of my birthday serving a seven-course meal to a family of ten. Rather pathetically, I had a lump in my throat the entire evening. I only stayed a few weeks. They didn't pay me and I stole the money I needed to get the train back to England.

When I arrived home the landscape had changed from the lush greens of spring to dirt-brown drought as far as the eye could see. Elton John and Kiki Dee were at number one with 'Don't go breaking my heart'—she in cheerful playschool dungarees and him a closet queen. It would have been helpful to lost and lonely young gay souls if people like Elton John could have found the courage to come out, instead of parading their excruciating pretence of heterosexuality on our television screens.

Back home with the scent of failure gathering around me I found a job at the Department of Employment as a clerical officer, where I sat opposite Peter, a Cambridge graduate with a first class degree in languages. He spoke six, fluently, but had not been able to find any other employment on account of his membership of the

Communist party. When Pete explained Marxism to me, it made complete sense of my life.

I joined the Communist Party and Pete fell in love with me and asked me to marry him and go with him to live in East Germany. While I was enthralled by the explanatory power of Marxist philosophy I wasn't daft enough to think this a wise course of action. I'd never so much as kissed the man and here he was professing undying love. Men were incredibly easy to get. Also, I was still seeing the motorbike salesman, who had managed to hang on to his boyfriend role in spite of my absences and casual cruelty to him. He was bemused by my political leanings and he feared my intellectual commie suitor, so we argued almost constantly.

I was locked in almost permanent battle with my dad too. I found his race hatred absolutely repulsive and at the time had limited ability to delve into the socio-psychological causes of it. I suspect that I was transferring my repulsion at his homophobia onto racism because this was a more intellectual than visceral pursuit. I might have drawn attention to my own hidden queerness if I'd punched him, as I dearly wanted to, when he sneered: 'Look at they fuckin queers', while watching Bowie and Mick Ronson performing their fabulous iconic duet on 'Starman'.

I finally decided to leave the family home after we'd had a screaming argument about race. He'd been watching something on television about Martin Luther King and come to the conclusion that 'They blackies 'ull rule this fuckin' planet in the next twenty five year, you mark ma wuds.'

This was a red rag to a bull and I'd, rather pointlessly, taken him on over it. Whenever we argued I looked at him like he was a piece of dog-shit on my shoe and I spoke to him with the attitude that he was beneath my contempt. Later that night, after he'd been to the pub and I was in bed, I heard a commotion outside my bedroom door. A few seconds later the door flung open and a terracotta plant pot containing a large Begonia landed on my pillow, inches from my head. This was somewhat reminiscent of the suitcase that nearly brained my sister Gerry years earlier. He was a creature of limited imagination when it came to alienating his daughters.

The next day I found a room to rent in a shared house and moved out.

The Alibi

The shared house was a massive old Georgian building that had once been a fine old family home but, by 1977, had been badly converted into a ramshackle collection of bedsits with a freezing cold bathroom on each floor. The ground floor was occupied by three Irishmen and I shared the second floor with four nurses. It is widely accepted that Irishmen know how to party, but those nurses made them look like the Temperance Society. These women thought nothing of pilfering whatever they could lay their hands on from their drug-trolley rounds and merrily swilled it down with a bottle of vodka on any average weekday night. The weekends were a blur of alcohol and amphetamine.

The motorbike salesman was nearly always around. He still lived at home but we were at an age where someone having their own place was a massive draw, especially when you're one of eleven kids. He'd become increasingly straight-laced and I was hiding my occasional drug use from him as well the three or four other boyfriends that I was seeing at the time. My life was a web of half-truths and obfuscations. He saw what he wanted to see. The nurses, for example, he thought a good influence on me because they had respectable steady jobs.

One Friday night we were in the pub with the Irish guys talking about marriage. As a joke I said to my boyfriend, 'You'd never marry me.'

'I would, next week if you like,' he replied.

On the Monday morning he went to the registry office, without telling me, and got a special license for the following Friday. I had less than five days. Everyone in the house was carried away with the 'romance' of it all and I was an immature attention seeking little idiot with far less brains than I was born with. We told our family and friends. I bought a new outfit and we married on the 1st of July, three weeks before my nineteenth birthday.

Having a husband was great heterosexual camouflage for me because I'd become adept at avoiding having sex with him. Also, because he was an immutable figure in the background, I could enjoy the flattery and constant self-affirmation I craved from other men without having sex with them by using my husband as my alibi. Being married to him further facilitated this subterfuge.

I was still in a place where being a lesbian had not occurred to me as an option. It wasn't a choice that I understood I could make.

The wedding was a miserable transaction, echoing my own parents shabby little marriage but without the defence of pregnancy. Afterwards we went to my mum and dad's flat for ham sandwiches and Victoria sponge and someone took a few snaps. I'm biting my lip in most of them and almost hiding behind other people. Certainly I wished I wasn't there. Later that night, back at the shared house, we had an impromptu party with our housemates and several people from the pub, one of whom was a man I'd been seeing. He'd turned up, not realising I had married that day, and tried to slow dance with me whilst entreating me to go for a spin in his new E-type jaguar. One of the Irishmen hit him over the head with a broom handle in defence of my new spouse's honour. It was all a ridiculous farce.

My husband and I moved into a place of our own and I carried on with my chaotic existence. My taste for amphetamines expanded in direct proportion to the growing sense I had of my lesbianism. Funding my fondness for speed was difficult with a husband controlling the purse strings, so I had 'boyfriends' who just happened to be dealers. Things weren't looking good for me overall. If anyone had been taking bets, I reckon the clever money would've been on 'junkie whore and dead before thirty'.

The Things You Do

I'd told my husband that I thought I was gay but he didn't believe me. Instead he thought I was unhappy because I hadn't finished my education and he offered to support me through 'A' levels. This was generous of him but his 'altruism' also tied me to him in gratitude.

I began studying English, History and Sociology at the F.E. College in September of 1979. I loved academic study and at twenty-one had more of a sense of the value of it than I would have done earlier. Of course, I fancied my English teacher like crazy and this had a salutary effect on the quality of my essays. In fact, she suggested that I should think about sitting the Oxbridge exam on the strength of a stonking good essay I'd written on Evelyn Waugh's 'A Handful of Dust'. It's amazing how desire can sharpen the wits.

But, in my despondency surrounding my sexuality, I was still taking too many bathtub blues and abrading my molars whilst cleaning behind the taps with a cotton bud in the middle of the night.

During this period I'd become friendly with my husband's sister, Jackie the witch, who had by now left her junkie husband. My husband had a distinct lack of familial affection and he was particularly suspicious of this outlandish sister. She and I got along like a house on fire. She had all manner of weird and wonderful mates.

Unlike her brother, she did believe I was a lesbian and offered to introduce me to a 'bisexual' witch friend of hers and to come with me to The Princess Royal, Northampton's only gay pub. I'd been longing to go there but feared that such an act would prove irrevocable.

On a Saturday night just before Christmas, Jackie took me to visit the bisexual witch. She was a fifty-something faded beauty with raven black dyed hair. She gave me tea and invited me into her parlour to read my Tarot cards. As she turned each card she talked about 'emotional journeys' and the 'difficult process of renewal'. At the end she took my hands in hers and intoned, 'My dear, you must find a nice little straight girl—and make her gay.'

Armed with this intelligence, Jackie and I left and went to the Princess Royal. It was small and packed, and after the pub shut there was a private members club upstairs. Jackie and I got signed in by a pair of elderly gay men and within the hour I'd been picked up by a gorgeous young lesbian called Jane. She had blonde hair and smelled heavenly. Jane had the kind of confidence born of being at the centre of a crowd of outsiders. She lived with two bitchy gay men who protected her like vituperative mother hens. She'd had every available lesbian in a fifty mile radius. Jane knew exactly what she wanted, and that was an older straight woman who had been her 'affair' then rejected her for the security of heterosexuality. In those days gays used 'affair' as a noun defining the person rather than the activity. There was, to me, something powerfully exotic about this affectation. I wanted to be an 'affair'.

I took Jane back to my marital home and we had sex on the living room floor. She scratched my back to ribbons. The next morning my husband woke us up. He opened the living room door, and then closed it again. Jane gathered up her clothes and fled into the morning. My husband, seething with barely controlled rage and disgust, told me to get out of the house. He was actually vomiting into the kitchen sink as I packed a suitcase and left. I went to my parents' for the holidays and I had a date with Jane for New Year's Eve.

My spirit soared with the sense of freedom and joy I felt as I hauled my luggage to Mum and Dad's council flat in Jimmy's End. As I passed a pub, 'Brass in Pocket' came blaring out of the door. It went to number one that week.

The date didn't go so well. Jane, it transpired, was far too much in love with the older straight woman and barely spoke to me all evening. She didn't protest when at 2am I said I'd walk home. That was a bitter cold night and, alone in the dark streets, I foresaw that this queer thing wasn't going to be plain sailing.

Leaving my husband also meant I'd have to leave college and get a job. This I did, and by the middle of January I'd secured a post in the Personnel Department at the County Council. On the strength of the expected salary, I also took a room in a house. It was tiny and bleak with a single bed and a Formica table but it was better than staying with my parents. My dad had stopped drinking by this time and was far less confrontational with me, but I needed to be alone to explore my shiny new sexual orientation and I wasn't yet ready to tell them about it.

The job was just another office, but I worked opposite a lovely, ethereal young woman called Wendy. We quickly became allies in the office politics game. We also shared a sense of humour, so we spent much of the day pissing ourselves about the bizarre lives and habits of our colleagues.

I was burning an entire box of candles at every end. Being the new lesbian on a very small block meant I was quickly snapped up by those more seasoned dykes around town. The 'scene' for women in those days revolved around the home of a woman called Pat. She'd been a dolly-bird of the sixties and was still absolutely stunning—think of the young Joanna Lumley and you'd not be a million miles away. She shared this home with the even more beautiful Helen, who drove an MG sports car and entertained an international string of gorgeous young women. Pat was the second woman I slept with and, while the encounter was dull, it was illuminating in that we both bore the scarred backs of recent encounters with Jane.

There were parties and clubs on three or four nights a week. Sometimes we piled into Pat's beetle and went to one-nighters in random small-town locations, and sometimes we went to that famous lesbian cellar, the 'Gateways' in Chelsea. There are some things about being old that are rubbish but I'm eternally glad that I'm old enough to say I went to 'The Gates'. It was run in the 'sixties by a butch dyke called Smithy and she still presided at the bar accepting gin from her grateful clientele. This is sheer lesbo memorabilia, but Dusty Springfield used to go to Gateways, so of course I'm proud to say I went there. As lesbians, we have so little historical connection that you really have to get it where you can.

Several mornings each week I arrived at work straight from the night before with the strains of 'Echo Beach' still ringing in my head. Wendy invariably covered for me when I was late or when I couldn't see straight from exhaustion. She knew about, and totally accepted, my lesbianism. She herself was in strange relationship with a hippy bloke called Geoff who had a couple of kids by another woman. Wendy seemed to spend a lot of time looking after those kids. She also spent a lot of time with other 'cool' sounding friends, in particular a couple called Phyllis and Alan who had a baby. Alan was trying to make it as a writer. This meant they were severely skint and Wendy tried to help out, buying baby clothes and little treats that she'd come and show me in the office.

Wendy said we should go out sometime, if I ever had a free evening. We arranged to go for a drink and our office chatter deepened into real friendship. We just never shut up from seven until they threw us out at midnight. We kissed on the cheek when we said goodbye and Wendy took my hand and squeezed it tight.

It wasn't long before I got chucked out of my horrible little room for having unnatural relationships. The landlady had found some semi-naked conquest of mine on the landing and I got my marching orders the following day. I had to go back to Mum and Dad's for a spell. While I was there I came down with some bug, probably bought on by too much partying and was off work for a week. Wendy came to visit me on the Tuesday night. She bought a bag of oranges and 'The Pretenders' new album. We ate the oranges and played the album in my bedroom. She told me that she'd lost her appetite because she was in love. I had noticed that she'd lost a lot of weight and idiotically asked who the lucky guy was. We were sitting on the floor leaning against my bed. She looked at me long and closed her beautiful eyes. Wordlessly we kissed and in our embrace ended on my bed where we made love silently with the muffled sound of 'Minder' coming from the telly in the living room.

We were head-over-heels in love. Everything was shining and golden, and the springtime around us just exploded. I started to live at Wendy's flat most of the time. She had broken up with the hippy and he'd left claiming to be happy that Wendy had 'found herself'. I realized that I needed now to tell my family that I was gay. This was a proper relationship and it was the first time I'd been in love.

I went to see my mum the next Saturday lunchtime. Dad was in the living room watching Grandstand. She busied around me making cheese-on-toast and I said, 'Mum, I've met someone and I'm in love.'

'Ooh, that's good,' she replied. 'What's his name?'

'Her name's Wendy, Mum. I'm a lesbian'

She layered the cheese on the bread thoughtfully and said, 'Oo, ere Deb. The things you do.'

Gerry (II)

The living person I most admire is my sister Gerry and she was the second person in my family I told. She was pleased and relieved, I think, because she'd been worried about my drug taking and this revelation explained my unhappiness. Gerry was savvy enough to realise what was going on with me and had tried to give me sisterly advice about the folly of drugs. In fact the amphetamines just stopped, virtually overnight. Of course, I still smoked dope and indulged in the occasional line of coke but it wasn't problem drug-taking.

At about this time Gerry was herself coming out of a long and difficult period of her life. She'd got rid of her useless alcoholic husband Cliff a couple of years previously and had met a new man, Mick. He was an unlikely choice, but he was steady, hardworking and prepared to take on her three kids. He'd had a rough ride himself.

Gerry's life with Cliff had been one of grim and unrelenting poverty laced with violence. She'd fallen pregnant again quite soon after they were married and had a boy, called John, after Cliff's alcoholic dad. The young family had moved out of the bedsitting room and into a condemned property in Devonshire Street. It was to be demolished to make way for a new block of flats. So the woman who owned the house was happy to let it out at thirty shillings a week for the duration of its existence. Additionally, it meant that Gerry would qualify for a council property when the houses finally came down. It was a ghastly place, a two-up two-down with an old back kitchen and plenty of scurrying wildlife.

Cliff never once held down a job and they eked out a living from the National Assistance Bureau and his petty criminal activities. He and his cronies broke into the corner shop on a fortnightly basis. Sometimes he seemed to have plenty of cash and would buy mad extravagant things but mostly they were penniless to the point of hunger. At this time Gerry tipped the scales at just over six stones. Cliff was rarely at home and Gerry was left alone in the horrible house with her baby. The one good thing that came from living there was that Gerry met her lifelong friend, Sandra, who lived at the end of the terrace. She was another young mother, and the two of them supported each other through years of poverty, most of the time helpless with laughter.

The street had been built in the 1840s on the site of a monastery that had been routed during the reformation and all the monks had been slaughtered. Most of the neighbours reported strange happenings and Gerry's house was no exception. Pots and pans would be flung about the kitchen in the middle of the night and ghostly figures drifted in and out of invisible cloisters. Sandra's radio came on of its own accord, and on a rare night out Gerry and Cliff had returned to petrified babysitters. The door to the parlour had been opening and closing all evening as if someone were coming in and out.

A particularly chilling incident involved John when he was just six months old. Gerry put the baby down in his cot for an afternoon nap, as was her habit. When he was fast asleep, she fastened the rails and went down the steep stairs to get on with chores in the kitchen. After fifteen minutes she went to check on the boy. He wasn't in his cot. Panic-stricken, she ran to the other bedroom but he wasn't there either. She ran downstairs and finally found the baby safe and still fast-asleep on the sofa in the parlour. The door to the room had been closed and latched and was awkward to undo. She took the baby in her arms and fled up the street to Sandra's house. Sandra had a huge Alsatian dog and they took him with them back to Gerry's place to investigate. As they neared the front door the dog's hair stood up on end and the animal skedaddled, not to be seen again that day. You may think that Gerry had simply forgotten where she'd left the baby. It is possible, but we know in our hearts that's not what happened.

In the time that she was with Cliff, Gerry had ten pregnancies, seven of which were miscarriages. One of these she lost during the year they lived in Devonshire Street. Gerry was in agony and losing blood and Sandra had phoned for a doctor. Cliff, as usual, was nowhere to be found. It was a bitter cold and snowy winter and the doctor couldn't get his car into the tiny narrow terrace. As a result he had slipped on the snow and arrived angry. This was, in fact, his usual condition. His name was Doctor Thompson and he was notorious for his unpleasant manners and general misogyny. He'd once given my mum a severe dressing down when she'd gone to him suspecting she had a prolapsed womb. He was disgusted that she must have been 'feeling inside' herself to have reached such a conclusion.

On this visit he refused to give Gerry any pain relief on the grounds that, 'Labour must be borne.'

He told Gerry to keep anything that 'came away' for later examination. Gerry lost the child that night. The next day she'd been able, with Sandra's help, to get herself downstairs and light a fire. Thompson arrived that evening and, giving the bloody lump that he'd instructed Gerry to keep a cursory glance, he tossed it into the open grate. Gerry watched as the burning mass unfurled, revealing, at its centre, her three-month-old foetus.

Eventually, the houses were demolished and Gerry did qualify for a council flat. Cliff made an unconvincing attempt at being a husband and father but it was short lived. He'd pretend that he was going to pay the rent on Friday each week and turn up again on Sunday, the money spent on booze and philandering. Eventually the rent arrears grew so much that Gerry was served an eviction notice. She was pregnant again when she was thrown out of the property with John, by this time a little boy of four. The few sticks of furniture she possessed were left standing in the street. She couldn't afford a van to take them away. Gerry stayed with Sandra, whose fortunes had been a little better than her own, until she got another house.

This new house wasn't up to much either, but beggars can't be choosers and the council had been reluctant to house her again anyway. She scraped together a few random oddments of furniture given through a local church: an oversized table, a lamp, an old rug, and bizarrely, a chaise lounge. She had no cooker or beds. By the time she moved in she had another child, a girl named Gail.

I must've been about twelve at this time and I spent loads of time at Gerry's place. She liked the company and I liked to be around her because there is something good and wise and decent in Gerry. She didn't have a telly so we sang songs to entertain each other. Gerry did a really mean version of 'Danny Boy' and I had a Beatles 'White Album' medley down to a tee, with a finale of 'Rocky Racoon'.

I would have done anything for her and it used to anger me beyond reason that she suffered so much, mostly for the want of a measly few quid. We worked out that just £500 would pay off all her debts and allow her to get the few bits she needed for her home. I'd have given anything to be in a position to get her that money. At twelve, all I could do was help her round up glass bottles so we could take them to the shop and get the deposits back. I pushed them up the street in an old pram and we scraped together enough for tea and a packet of fags.

The police had finally nailed Cliff for aggravated robbery and he served a year in prison. Gerry swore it was over with him, but when he came out she weakened again and took him back. He promised he'd learned his lesson and that from now on things would be different. This lasted a few months before he was back to his regular ways.

On one occasion when he beat her she called the police. He was so incensed by her action that he continued his assault after they arrived. Far from making an arrest, they left. As they walked up the street, Gerry impotently shouted after them, 'You cowardly bastards.'

There were no women's refuges at this time. There was nowhere to go. It is hard for a person raised in a world where domestic violence was an unremarked commonplace to break free of this cycle, especially so when children are involved. The aggressor in these cases has the opportunity to condition the victim, much as in the Nazi concentration camps. Abuse is systematic and forms an integral part of the relationship dynamic. Victims lose hope and self-esteem and thus the ability to challenge.

It took another few years until Gerry developed the strength to fight her feelings for Cliff. In 1974 she went into hospital to be sterilised and during the operation they found she was pregnant again. Before this tenacious child was born she finally threw Cliff out. She didn't love him anymore.

In spite of the fact that she no longer lived among the clamorous monks in Devonshire Street, Gerry still had ghosts. She is an incredibly empathic human being and I think that her sense of others is a kind of opening through which a more developed awareness of the paranormal can flow. For example, she frequently had lucid dreams. She became conscious when she was dreaming and possessed the ability to control the dream state. When this happened, she would fly across England above the patchwork fields to Torquay. It was here she had spent a weekend with Sandra and their respective men. It was the happiest time she could remember.

One night after Cliff had gone she awoke from dreaming that someone was in her bedroom, standing in the corner. She had lain awake for several moments peering into the darkened room, when a phone began to ring. She didn't have a phone line, and she realised with dawning terror that it was Gail's toy phone ringing on the landing. She hid beneath the covers where she stayed until light came through the thin curtains.

Life's Rich Pageant

I have an image of Wendy engraved on my mind's eye. She is dancing at the Princess Royal to the Pretenders hit 'Talk of the Town' in her torn Levi's and hippy tea-shirt, long dark hair a curtain in front of her face, entirely lost in music.

'You've changed your place in this world.'

She was a beautiful woman and she was my girlfriend. I had found a nice little straight girl and I had made her gay.

It quickly became apparent that her ex-boyfriend Geoff was not so overjoyed at Wendy's new found happiness. In fact, he was insanely jealous and, worryingly, had in the past shown psychotic tendencies. During their relationship he wanted to get a massive Alsatian dog which Wendy, a collector of stray cats, didn't want. Geoff, in a bid to persuade her, arranged for a mate of his to break into Wendy's bedroom. She was so terrified by the event that she agreed to the attack dog. She only found out later that he'd orchestrated the whole affair.

Wendy and I were pretty much living together at the flat she had shared with Geoff, and to which he still had a key. We were extremely vulnerable. Wendy's friends Alan and Phyllis became alarmed as Geoff's behaviour got increasingly unpredictable and Alan came over to insist we pack a few things and come to stay at their place. It was the first time I'd met the couple that I'd heard Wendy talk about at work and I was overwhelmed with the open generosity they showed towards me.

We packed a bag and walked with Alan back to their house and bought a drink at the off-licence on the way. Alan talked about books and art and played brilliant albums all evening that I'd never heard before: John Cale, David Ackles and Lewis Fury. He also played 'The Hissing of Summer Lawns' and to my mind you can always trust a man who likes Joni Mitchell. Phyllis was less loquacious, but when she spoke it was with startlingly perceptive observations and rapier wit. I was totally out of my depth intellectually so I sat quiet and listened and hoped I wouldn't come across as rude. One thing I did know though, was that I'd found some people who made me feel less lonely—people who were prepared to challenge the way of things and who wanted a better, more loving world.

Wendy and I continued to work at the County Council but our relationship was a little too rich for the confines of a small office. I'm only guessing, but I think when we gazed across our desks and fed each other Camembert and grapes for lunch that some of our colleagues may have twigged that our friendliness had blossomed into something less than wholesome.

By September, they'd had all they could stomach and we were called into the chief executive's office and told that one of us was to be made redundant. We could decide between us who it should be. We waited until payday, picked up our checks and never went back.

By that time we'd secured our own flat, so we both signed on the dole and spent the winter in love.

Our friendship with Phyllis and Alan continued to grow. We spent loads of time with Phyllis and their two year old, Leah, while Alan hammered away at the typewriter upstairs in their bedroom, crafting comic book stories and staring to get some recognition. Phyllis was pregnant with their second child and we spent many a winter evening making up daft names for the baby.

In February 1981, Wendy and I were awoken in the middle of the night by the sound of something soft hitting the bedroom window. It was Alan's gloves. This is the kind of thing people did before phones became a part of the human anatomy. Phyllis was in the early stages of labour and we had to go to their house to look after Leah while they went to the maternity hospital. Next morning at 8am Alan stuck his head round the bedroom door and said, 'It's a girl and she's called Amber.'

Wendy and I drifted back to sleep. Next I was awakened by Leah sitting on my throat, prizing my eyelids apart with small sticky fingers and thrusting her book in front of them. Leah and Amber would be the closest I would come in life to having children myself.

Phyllis and Alan's house was a centre for Northampton's hipsters. Would-be artists, musicians, feminists and radical intellectuals hung out there. Most of them eventually got proper jobs and became slaves to Capitalism, me included, but at the time it felt like home. Alan, of course, never did get a proper job.

With the turn of the season into spring, Wendy and I decided to get summer jobs and save up so we could do some travelling later in the year. We saw an advert for two people to help run a camp-shop on the Isle of Wight. It seemed ideal, we'd be working together and the arrangement was 'all found' so we could save everything we earned.

Our boss was a wiry little man called Mr Peplow. An ex-serviceman, he ran the camp with military precision. We worked a stupid and probably illegal amount of hours under the watchful eye of the shop manager, Eric. He reported everything back to Mr Peplow and had a fondness for aphorisms, his favourite being 'It's all in life's rich pageant', which he'd accompany with a circular sweep of his arms and a beatific smile.

Three mornings a week we were also joined by a local woman called Paddy. She'd got stuck in 1967, a casualty of 'the summer of love', and wafted around in a hippy dress and big floppy hat.

Underlying the peace and love vibe though was the darkness of encroaching mental illness. Paddy became obsessed with Wendy and me. Being gay in a world where it was still outré attracted its share of weirdoes in the spirit of: I'm a crazy outsider, just like you. Being on the Isle of Wight only intensified this phenomenon. Paddy wanted to engulf us with love and home-baked brownies. We just wanted to earn some money and get off the Island as soon as possible. We were joined in this aim by Paddy's husband who felt threatened by us and wanted to ensure Paddy remained imprisoned in their chocolate-box cottage. No doubt Paddy was a troubled soul but the husband somehow liked it that way. This unhappy relationship seemed to embody my own sense of confinement on the Island.

Wendy had plans to write. She wanted to write children's books about a bear called Menjim and his wife Mae. Obviously writing was not going to pay the rent, so alongside this ambition she also planned to start a market-stall business selling second hand children's clothes. She went to every jumble sale on the Island and collected a huge amount of kid's stuff to re-model and sell at a profit. She also knitted tiny perfect matinee jackets in vibrant stripes. Kid's clothes at the time were a drab monotony of pale pink and blue, so I could see the potential of selling stuff that was a bit original.

I started to feel a prick of concern when her jumble sale purchases became so voluminous that we would have had to rent a van to get it off the Island. We were supposed to be going travelling so this didn't add up. I also felt it was somehow my responsibility to organise the shipment and storage of this stuff.

Things started to fall apart when Peplow didn't pay us the four months he owed at the end of August. This was the money we needed to go travelling. I went to his office at the beginning of September to ask him what had happened to our wages. This scumbag went puce with anger and bellowed, 'Get out of my office and off this campsite you filthy queer and take your pervert friend with you.'

I gathered this meant we weren't getting paid. Wendy and I skipped the Island that night with what we could carry of our stuff. We never got the money. We didn't go travelling.

Back in Northampton, we rented a miserable room in a gloomy, ugly, cold and haunted house. It had long narrow corridors where imagined ghosts chased you into a run. At the end of one of these was a massive shared bathroom with a toilet in one corner and a shabby old bath in another. Its cracked chequered linoleum stretched infinitely away as you sat, agoraphobic, on the bog. The janitor in this hovel murmured to himself and had a metal calliper on his leg that clanked and creaked as he mounted the stairs. His noisy rambling around the house punctuated our evenings.

We knew the house was haunted because Phyllis and Alan had lived in the room below ours before they married. Phyllis had been awakened one night by Alan sitting up in bed saying 'Please leave' to the ether. He could see a little Victorian girl standing in the middle of the room who simply faded away.

The house stood in a row of very fine, nicely proportioned town houses yet managed itself to be a huge windowless monstrosity. It's a measure of the nastiness of the place that it was demolished in the 1990's and a small neat bungalow now stands incongruously in its place.

I got a job managing a video shop and Wendy carried on collecting baby clothes and knitting. The room gradually filled up with black plastic sacks full of jumble. One entire wall was made of bin bags. She showed no sign of getting the market stall thing organised. We started to argue.

After a few months the council came through with a flat on one of the new estates on the eastern edge of town. Gerry arrived as we were loading the removal van with a set of saucepans for us and Mum and Dad bought a cheap carpet and came up to fit it. Dad smoked a fag and admired his handy-work, while Mum bustled about finding a kettle to make tea. I started to feel sad about them. Wendy filled the spare room with the, by now, ominous bin bags. Our arguments grew fierce. Our good times receded.

I left the video shop job and got three different bar jobs and a laundry round. I drove round the county picking up laundry on a Monday morning and delivering it back on the Thursday. One of my calls was at Althorpe House. We laundered the Spencer family bed-linen. Charles and Diana had only recently married and the country was still enthralled by the fairy tale romance. Whenever the couple had stayed at her country seat the women at the laundry examined the sheets for signs of the royal emissions, like medieval ladies in waiting.

I also got to take the transit van home, which I used to do light removals on the side. I kept busy, and although I knew the crazy-in-love thing with Wendy had deserted me, I was happy.

For the first time I felt in control. I made my own money, had some good mates and, most important, I could be exactly who I wanted to be. I decided to change my name. Having little regard for my paternity, I had taken my husband's surname when we married. Clearly, I could not spend the rest of my life bearing the name of a man I would never see again and neither did I see any sense in reverting to my dad's name. I considered Munroe, my Mum's maiden name, but everyone would have thought it was about Marilyn and that seemed goofy. I wanted alliteration with 'D' and, in the end, I stuck a pin in an atlas. Delano is a town in California named for the 'D' in Franklin D Roosevelt.

Wendy and I decided to split up. I took her and her gear without recriminations to her sister's place. My first love had gone. I went back to the flat and cried my mascara off. I was in the process of re-doing it ready to go to one of my tedious bar jobs when a knock came to the front door. It was my good friend, Jamie, brandishing an unopened bottle of tequila and a wrap of chemical solace.

'Come in,' said I. 'Didn't fancy work much anyway.'

After our break-up I still saw Wendy, but with distance I realised her great emotional fragility. Her conversation was dotted with strange innuendo and her mannerisms seemed changed. What had once seemed merely idiosyncratic had shifted into something almost menacing.

She had begun dating a man and gradually drifted away from me and her circle of friends.

I have another, more disturbing, abiding image of her. She had volunteered to take part in a hair-dressing show. I was waiting tables at the do, along with a group of random town dykes. What I hadn't realised was that she'd agreed to have her head completely shaved. The young hairdresser on stage, not the greatest practitioner in the first place, had calmed his nerves with vodka and amphetamines and his hand was unsteady with the razor. By the time he'd finished, Wendy's poor shaved head was cut to ribbons and bleeding. Her gorgeous hair lay in drifts around the chair. It was this that broke my heart. Not because she was no longer beautiful, she was, but because I knew this action was more than lovable eccentricity. She was lost to me more profoundly than I'd realised.

La Mama Morta

Eventually I did go travelling.

A couple of years after Wendy and I split, I gave up the council flat and went through Europe to Greece with another lover. We slept on the black volcanic-sand beach at Thira and hopped across the Islands of the Aegean. I kept a journal of my travels and in it I also recorded dreams. It is for this reason that I have such recall of this particular dream.

I am in the house of my childhood. In the corner of the room my mother is sitting on a chair hunched, impossibly small and old and frail. I go to her and lift her in my arms and, carrying her into the street, I cry out to the heavens 'Who has done this?'

'You have,' replies a voice from the heavens.

This was recorded on June 10th 1984.

By August we had washed up on the gay island of Mykonos and had been joined by a crew of Northampton dykes on their annual fortnight holiday. My lover and I were planning to go on to Lesbos when our mates went home, then maybe east to Turkey and the Black Sea.

We'd been swimming in the sea and drinking beer in a beach taverna. Some of us decided to climb the steep path up the hill behind the beach. My girlfriend stayed at the taverna. As we started walking back down I saw her, a dot at the bottom of the hill, running up towards me. I knew with absolute certainty that something was wrong. I ran down to meet her.

'Calm down, calm down,' she was saying urgently as we came within earshot.

'Just tell me,' I yelled. 'Is it my mum?'

'Yes,' she said trying to hold me. 'You have to phone home.'

I collapsed to my knees and screamed. A kind of primal howling escaped my lungs.

My girlfriend had decided to call her parents while I was gone. My family had left messages asking for me to get in touch with everyone they knew we might contact. I got back to the taverna and phoned Martin. He sounded desolate. Mum had been diagnosed with inoperable cancer. She'd been given six months to live.

We got the next boat back to Athens and from there a flight to London. Martin picked us up from Heathrow. He was heartbroken. His pain was palpable. He and I had loved her more than we would ever now be able to say or show. The family had been advised by the consultants at the hospital not to tell her she was dying. I have always doubted the wisdom of this.

When I saw my mum she cried in my arms and said: 'Ar noo ar shud roar when ar seen ere Deb.'

She actually lived another gruelling eighteen months. Her condition gradually deteriorated as the disease more and more depleted her body. Dad was unequal to the task of dealing with either the situation or his feelings. In spite of their less than perfect marriage, he'd loved her in the best way he could. In the final weeks of her life, Mum told us he'd become deranged with grief and had attacked her in the night when he'd woken up disoriented. It was decided that one of us would have to stay at their flat to protect her. This duty fell to me. It turned out to be the last night she would be at home and the last time I would ever speak to her. Dad became aggressive in the small hours and I'd got Mum up to sit with me in the living room. She was uncomfortable lying down. She begged me to tell her that she wasn't going to die. I maintained the lie. I told her she would live.

The next morning she was taken to the hospice where she spent a week without regaining consciousness. Gerry had arranged to marry her new man Mick and they bought the wedding forward in the hope that the news of the event would bring Mum to us again for a last few words. It didn't.

She slipped from the opiate coma into death in the night. Dad was asleep in the visitor's room.

She will always live inside me.

Last Words

Jerry could not deal with his grief and lashed out at us all with anger and blame. He smashed every piece of crockery in the flat and put it all in a biscuit tin. He kept one mug and one plate. It was all, he said, he would need now that she was gone. I doubted he'd survive, but he did, albeit in a kind of smoke-filled council flat limbo. As the years went by the tobacco stains that yellowed the walls escaped and curled out of his letter box and down the front door. He smoked filter-tips by now—to him this was virtually giving up. It is this image of him in his armchair with his fags and cup of tea, taken by Phyllis on a Polaroid camera that appears, almost unaltered, in Alan's unfinished work 'Big Numbers'.

Jerry began to speak of my mother as a saint and completely rewrote the history of their strange marriage to fit his fantasy. No one contradicted him.

His attitude to the world in general and women in particular changed not at all. He would meet Mick, Gerry's sweet and faithful new husband, for a cup of tea at the community centre and suggest to him that he 'knock the hat off' a simple-minded woman who worked there. I know this is wrong, but in my family we actually find this funny. It's the sort of memory that makes us all fall about laughing when we reminisce. Dad adored Gerry. She was the apple of his eye but he saw no contradiction there. To him, marital fidelity had no meaning. As long as a couple pooled their resources, that was commitment. This is the socialisation of the Gorbals.

In fact, his horrible sexual predilections featured in the repetitive tale he'd relate about an incident he'd supposedly witnessed in town concerning 'big black boys' and 'gurls wi' skirts awae up tae their arses.' He would re-tell this story nearly every time I visited with slightly different plot twists each time. I wouldn't have minded, but he did it in front of my friends who'd been brave enough to volunteer to accompany me on these dreaded encounters.

On one occasion when Phyllis had come with me – and bear in mind she is a feminist intellectual – he told me, as he usually did to 'Put the kettle on Genie.' This was a name he gave to all women.

Bad enough you might think, but no, worse was to come.

‘Aye an’ gi’ it tae yer pal in ma sex positions mug.’

He had taken the vile object, which was indeed a mug decorated with an astrological array of sex positions, out of the cabinet and was handing it to Phyllis for her perusal and entertainment before I could get into the living room and somehow intervene.

Phyllis - in Jerry’s sitting room

He was, though, generous to a fault. He routinely stole tins of salmon from the Co-op which he’d try to press upon anyone who called. He didn’t even eat fish. This was just the most luxurious item he could imagine. Whenever Leah and Amber came to his flat with me he offered them whatever he’d got in his cupboard.

‘Ye want a banana,’ he’d shout at them. ‘Ye want a yogurt.’

They were simply bemused by him.

He lived another twelve years after Dorothy died. By this time I was teaching in London. I got a call to come up to Northampton General Hospital from Gerry’s daughter Gail. He was on his last legs. Amazingly, he didn’t have lung cancer; his lungs had simply packed up through seventy years of smoking.

When I arrived at the hospital, all of my siblings were there with their respective partners and some of the grandchildren. The room was crowded. Dad was rasping out his last few breaths unconscious of us all. It’s hard to make conversation in such circumstances, and after I’d been updated on his demise we fell to wondering how long he'd got and if it was wise for us all to stay. The partners and grandchildren began to drift away and, by midnight, we had decided to take turns. Gerry, Chris and I would do the night and Martin was dispatched to get some sleep and return for the morning shift.

At around 3am Dad's rasping breath began to falter. Then it stopped. Chris went to the nurses' station and came back with the kind and competent black nurse who'd been popping her head around the door occasionally. She leaned over him to check his breath and felt for a pulse. Suddenly he struggled, sat bolt upright and bellowed out what turned out to be his last words: 'Get that black cunt awae fae me.'

It took all four of us to hold him down to the bed. We managed to quiet the old bastard down and fortunately the nurse, with incredible grace, showed no sign of being on the receiving end of his racist abuse. All we could do was apologise weakly and thank her profusely.

The rest of the night continued in this vein with him drifting in and out of consciousness. Martin arrived back at seven in the morning and we girls went to freshen up.

At four that afternoon, Gerry and I were alone in the room with him when his breathing stopped again. We looked at each other and decided without words not to fetch anyone until we were sure he was dead. When we were satisfied that this was the case, Gerry went to fetch another nurse who pronounced him dead. We both cried. Gerry cried because she had loved him. I cried for the waste and the unhappiness that need not have been, and probably from exhaustion.

His funeral passed without incident. Afterwards at the funeral home, where tea and sandwiches were served, someone remarked that Gerry's youngest lad Matthew was the spitting image of our dad. As general agreement was being murmured by all, our cousin piped up and in a questioning tone said, 'I don't think he looks *dead*, like yer dad.'

My siblings and I howled and sobbed with laughter. We had to hold our sides and rock with mirth. The assembled company looked askance, but still we could not stop.

After our hilarity had subsided we had to avoid looking at each other for fear of another outbreak. I feel sure the guests and staff at the home saw it as our way of expressing grief. It was nothing of the kind. We can take the piss at anything, and laughing till we weep is the cement in our relationship. Whatever our mum and dad did wrong, this was the precious gift they gave us.

Political Shenanigans

Phyllis got me interested in Green politics during the 1980s. I'd flirted with socialist political affiliations before but when she showed me the green manifesto it made perfect sense. It remains the only sensible and logical way to sustain a decent and humane way of life on Earth.

The Ecology Party was in the process of changing its name to The Green Party when I joined in 1985. In Northampton they were a motley crew of middle-class do-gooders. They met weekly in someone's house to make strategy decisions on whether to hold a cake sale or a coffee morning to raise funds. No one else came to these events so they made £4.27 from eating each other's organic fruit cake to plough back into the party purse. It obviously wasn't going to 'show Thatcher'.

Phyllis and I, rather arrogantly, decided to 'put a rocket under them'. We started attending these meetings, swelling the numbers by a third, and making suggestions for more effective ways to make money and publicise the cause. We began putting on gigs in the back room of a town pub.

This worked well for the local musicians because they got their expenses and a gig, which we publicised locally, as well as the kudos of being involved in this 'hip' fledgling political movement. For its part, the party got the association with youth culture and we attracted comparatively large numbers of people to the shows. Phyllis and I took money at the door, so if people showed any interest we got the opportunity to talk about green politics.

Alan did the posters advertising the gigs, which we printed up in black and white and then hand-coloured with felt tips. Leah and Amber helped in this department. Then we fly-posted the town with them. One of our best posters was for a band called 'Big'. Alan had done a gorgeous image of a huge fat man literally tearing his heart out. We coloured the heart and blood that dripped from it in indelible red pen. It gave us no end of pleasure that the red heart adorned the nooks and crannies of Northampton for years after the posters had been ripped down.

We also made some money, enough in fact to get more involved in grassroots politics in general. When Kings Heath primary school was threatened with closure Phyllis and I went and talked to the parents committee and paid for a coach to take them to the houses of parliament to lobby government in aid of their cause. This was significantly more than the Labour Party was prepared to offer them.

By the time of the 1987 election we were ready to field a candidate for Northampton North. The obvious choice was Mike, the person who had set up the party years before in Northampton and who had worked tirelessly, if a little ineffectually, ever since in its cause. He was a bit of a drip but he lived the life and he was, sure as hell, a massive improvement on most of the grotesques that run for office. It took me by complete surprise when I was approached by two party members with an offer to 'ensure that I won the candidacy' and to 'give financial support to my campaign'. We clearly weren't going to win any elections – it's taken another twenty-five years to get a Green MP – but the principle of the thing was utterly corrupt. In embryo it was exactly what we despised in the other political parties.

The following week at the meeting to elect a candidate, I told the assembled members what had happened and named those involved. Everyone looked embarrassed, as if someone had farted. They were at a loss as to how to respond. Phyllis gallantly tried to explain why we saw this as crucial to the development of the party but her eloquence fell on deaf ears. In retrospect it's clear that they were happy with their cake sales and our revelations had upset the 'niceness' of everything.

We ended our association with the local party and, as it turned out, this was a timely move. At the Tory party conference that year Thatcher had started making ugly noises about homosexuality,

'We cannot have our children growing up believing that they have the inalienable right to be gay,' she bleated to massive applause from the gathered conservative degenerates. All the progress that gay people had made after decriminalisation in 1967 was about to be ripped away by a malevolent new clause in the local government bill dubbed 'Clause 28'. It was to this vile contrivance that we next turned our attention.

The clause aimed to outlaw 'the promotion of homosexuality', whatever that meant, and it called lesbian and gay parents 'pretended parents'. These peculiar terms have never had any viable meaning in law—they are too vague and too emotive. This is precisely what made the clause so effective. No one knew what it meant, so everyone could assume it meant them. Anyone of us might inadvertently 'promote' homosexuality or 'pretend' to be a parent.

I was in fact 'pretending' to be a parent to Leah and Amber and my invidious position was made abundantly clear to me one day when I tried to attend their parents evening. Amber's homophobic teacher refused to allow me entrance to the school and the head-teacher was summoned to intercede. He was a nasty little homophobe himself, and he turned a horrid shade of burgundy and threw himself bodily across the doorway to bar my entry. On another occasion, when I was collecting Amber from school in a torrential downpour, instead of making her run the fifty metres to the school gate and get soaked, I lifted her over the fence. Unbeknown to me, the head-teacher had outlawed such actions and had spotted me in this calumny. He raced out of the school and furiously screamed 'You're jeopardising the lives of all the children in my care.'

It summed up his attitude, about to be sanctioned by law, quite neatly.

***Leah** and **Amber** launch an attack*

Alan was, by 1987, celebrated as the 'doyenne of British comics'. He'd had brilliant and deserved success with a number of ground-breaking graphic novels. Through him, we had a great many connections with comic book artists and a little bit of know-how in terms of publishing. We decided to create a benefit comic to raise awareness and funds to fight the new law. The book would be called A.A.R.G.H. (Artists Against Rampant Government Homophobia). Alan produced a beautiful and moving lesbian and gay history in the form of a poem called 'The Mirror of Love' which featured as the lead piece. We had contributions from a diverse set of good people, the majority of whom were published writers and artists. It is always creators who are expected to give their time to such causes but in this instance Phyllis and I managed to inveigle the US distribution company to put the book out for free. This was unheard of. For a project of its kind we did well, selling 10,000 copies in Britain and the US. We made £10,000 for the Organisation for Lesbian and Gay Action.

Amber** and **Leah
- Section 28 demonstration

It was a frightening time to be gay. When Phyllis and I went to a protest march and rally in Kennington Park in London we were warned from the stage not to leave the park because individuals were being arrested as they made their way home. The charge being levelled was 'behaviour likely to cause a breach of the peace'. A political climate like this gives license to homophobes and attacks increased across the country. Councillor Brownhills, a Conservative, publicly called on his leader to: Gas the queers. Thatcher did nothing to indicate that this was not her own favoured solution. We did not stop the clause becoming Section 28 and entering the statute books in 1988.

It was eventually repealed in 2003. What was particularly pernicious was the fact that it was widely believed that teachers and schools should not 'promote' homosexuality. As a result, the very mention of it disappeared from the school curriculum.

The Inalienable Right to be Gay

When I began teaching in 1995 I was suddenly thrust amongst a culture of kids who wore their homophobia as a badge of honour and had their hatred enshrined in law. I worked in a tough, multi-cultural school in the London borough of Newham. As in most London schools, there was a good proportion of gay staff, but none of them was open with the kids. I had spent the previous fifteen years shoving my sexuality down peoples' throats, so retreating to the closet was an emotional iron cage to me. The very idea of coming out to students was thought to be insane, and most likely career suicide. Nonetheless the butch dykes and bitchy queens I counted among my mates on the staff did give me the support I needed to make that step, even though I know they feared that it might somehow expose them too.

I gave myself a year to build relationships with the kids, and then informed the head of my intention. To his credit he offered to support me, though his hunted expression betrayed his fears—namely Muslim parents and my line manager, Audrey, the Head of R.E., who was a fundamentalist Christian. She taught the kids that abortion was evil and was herself so fecund that she pumped involuntary breast milk, constantly staining her already grubby two-pieces.

I bided my time, waiting for an opportunity to come out 'naturally' rather than saying: 'Right everyone, pens down. I'm a lesbian.' My chance came during a PSHE lesson on equality. I had written some key words on the board, one of which was 'homosexual'.

'Why've we gotta learn abaht queers, Miss,' they chorused, amiably enough. They were, in the main, a nice bunch of kids.

'Because many people in our society are homosexual,' I replied.

'Nobody here's bent, Miss,' they claimed.

'I am,' I said.

There was silence. I watched one girl change colour: rose-pink to deathly grey. Then there was disbelief.

'No you're *not,* Miss. This is one of your role-play things.'

'No, really I am. I'm not kidding about this.'

A barrage of questions followed. I told them that I'd answer them as long as they didn't concern things I considered private, or other members of staff. What ensued was an open discussion about love, freedom, human rights and respect—and I have been privileged to have many such conversations with young people since then.

It wasn't until five minutes before the bell that one of the boys asked; 'So what do lesbians do in bed?'

I didn't need to reply: he was instantly slapped down by some hard-case girls for 'disrespecting Miss'. These same girls asked me if I wanted them to keep it a secret. So Rome wasn't built in a day—but I thanked them for their consideration, explaining that I'd given it a lot of thought, and the whole point was that I had nothing to hide.

In the weeks and months that followed there was a flurry of homophobic incidents. Some of the Afro-Caribbean boys, for example, simply could not accept that there should be an open homosexual in their midst. I spent a great deal of time with these young men equating homophobia with the racism that they experienced every day of their lives. I think that this may have made some impression. But clearly their cultural background and rigid sense of masculinity presented an almost impassable barrier to them. Over time, these incidents reduced in frequency. When kids quietly said 'lesbian' as they passed me in the corridor I always stopped and said: 'Yes, that's right—anything else you'd like to add?'

The worst case was Audrey, the aforementioned Head of RE. As soon as she discovered, not just my disgusting sexual preference, but the shocking fact that I'd revealed it to the students, she ceased to speak to, or even acknowledge, me. Lucky me—except we had to attend the same meetings and share resources. When finally I tried to approach her on a matter of school business and, mumbling 'pervert', she physically pushed me aside, I had no choice but to initiate a meeting with senior staff and union representatives. During this attempt to resolve our contretemps, Audrey began screaming at me, accusing me of 'sharing vile and filthy secrets with children'. I declined to respond and left the room. Now, I don't know what happened in my absence - maybe her God of Love intervened - but Audrey came to me later that day sobbing and begging forgiveness. Clearly the woman was unhinged, but something had shifted in her. From that day on she treated me with respect—one, I like to imagine, born of fear.

Now, it's the nature of the case that coming out is something one must do almost on a daily basis: new people, new forms to fill in and, for me, new schools and classes. In every school where I have subsequently taught I have made it my business to seek out and attack homophobia wherever I encounter it. It is a shocking fact that only six percent of schools in England have equality policies which include homophobia as a form of bullying—when it is, in fact, endemic in all schools. It is the last bastion of prejudice and it is allowed to flourish across our education system.

I have chipped away at this hatred by introducing new policies that include advancing to homosexuals the same rights enjoyed by the rest of the school. I have incorporated the concept into the school curriculum, trained staff in ways to deal with it their own classrooms, and I have raised displays of gay history. But, most importantly, I am out myself. This is not an easy position to occupy all the time, but to me it is infinitely preferable to allowing the perennial assumptions and prejudices to go unchallenged.

Martine

I had a series of relationships during the 1990s, varying from the merely ill-judged to the completely disastrous. The last of these was with a deeply homophobic P.E. dyke. When this debacle ended in 2000, I found myself homeless, jobless and adrift from my emotional moorings.

My friend Jamie came and rescued me from the house I shared with this woman—a role he has stoically rehearsed from time to time. Rather absurdly it was a picturesque cottage in Ironbridge which we jointly owned. I went to live with Phyllis in Liverpool while I repaired and re-assessed my life. She put up with my misery and night-time horrors without complaint. Leah and Amber were at university and the distraction of their comings and goings was curative. When Amber was home we had to share her bed. She's not a small girl, and often in the night she'd grab me, plump me up as if I were an old pillow and arrange herself around me. It helped to heal me and, gradually, I regained my equilibrium and extracted myself from the complicated financial mess I'd made.

Being a single lesbian outside of the capital is a tough call if you want to any sort of social life, and Liverpool in particular is a desert for lesbians. I decided I must move back to London if I was ever going to get laid again.

Another good friend of mine, Sue, was also moving to London at the same time and we decided to share a flat. We rented a first-floor, two-bed place above a kebab shop in Green Lanes. It was handy for the tube and had a bus stop right outside. In fact people on the top deck could actually watch our telly from the bus. When traffic was really slow, entire episodes of Eastenders could conveniently be viewed by passing commuters.

The first day I moved in, I ventured onto the balcony at the back which overlooked the Kebab shop yard. It was full of Turkish men hawking up phlegm and the lane at the rear was alive with rats. There was a whole discarded Pizza with a rat on top of it munching away at the Mozzarella and several others circling in anticipation. I am rat-phobic. The very sight of one on telly makes me physically shudder and bury my head inside my t-shirt. I immediately rang the landlord and told him I'd be moving out that day unless he did something about it. Within an hour a hero from Rentokil was on the doorstep. When he saw the extent of the problem he asked me if he could fetch his rifle. He shot about ten rats from the balcony of the flat and laid poison the length of the back lane and in the kebab shop yard. I never saw the rats again, though I fear my Karma will struggle to survive my sanctioning this mass extermination.

Sue and I embarked full-steam ahead on a London life. I wasn't looking for love and I didn't want to start another relationship. I was simply enjoying being a single lesbian.

Sue is heterosexual and on Saturday nights we alternated straight and gay pubs. We'd eaten at an Italian on Stroud Green Road and then had a pint in a straight pub where, much to Sue's chagrin, some bloke tried to chat me up. We left and went to The Flag on Crouch Hill. It was quiet for a Saturday and we were debating a trip into town when a couple of men and a woman came in.

They hadn't been in long before the woman caught my eye, and we did that glancing over at each other thing. Sue miserably resigned herself to not going into town and went to get another drink instead. As soon as she went to the bar the woman came over to me and introduced herself, in a divine French accent, as Martina. Having a French accent is a sure-fire way of getting English girls, and this, coupled with the deepest, darkest eyes in the entire world, was more than enough to win me over. We got chatting and her friends joined us.

They were a gay couple called Brian and Julian. Martina lived with them. We had a brilliant night. They were all intelligent, politically sound-as-a-pound and an excellent laugh. Martina was from the Auvergne, and had been living in London for the last six years. She wasn't actually called

Martina, but Martine. She had just got into the habit of not correcting English peoples' need to put an 'A' at the end of it, especially if only for a one night stand. At this point, that is what we both had in mind.

We invited them back to our flat and, in a match-making bid, Sue and the boys suggested that Martine and I share the first cab together. She claims I sat as far away from her as I could while she valiantly tried to snog me. I'd already decided to sleep with her and just didn't want to seem over-eager. When we got back to the flat Martine followed me into the kitchen and asked to see the balcony. She had plotted that it would be a romantic place to turn to me under the stars and take me in an embrace. Notwithstanding the rats and the Turkish men, this balcony had only ever been a strip of concrete giving access to the shed, so her Gallic passions were thwarted yet again. Eventually, it was me who kissed her against the fridge, back in the safety of the kitchen.

Brian and Julian, as it turned out, are a garrulous pair and we talked the night away. It was nearly five by the time they left. Martine stayed with me. We didn't sleep. When she left in the morning she asked for my phone number. I gave it, though I never expected to see her again.

She called me the following Thursday. I was at work and Sue took the message. 'That little Frenchie's phoned,' she said. 'I said you'd call her back.'

I did, and we met for a proper date that Saturday night. It was easy. Over the weeks and months that followed, I gradually gave up my 'I want to be single' pretence and gave in to the perfect simple fact that I'd met the woman I would spend the rest of my life with.

We got married in 2006. The government, under pressure from the church and the Tory faithful, have not yet deemed that 'civil partnership' be called marriage, and personally I don't give a monkeys what we call it. We got equal rights out of the deal and that's why we did it.

Marriage is a profoundly conservative institution anyway, and hopelessly embedded in patriarchy. Certainly the event itself bore all the hallmarks of a wedding. In the presence of our nearest and dearest, we promised to love, honour and respect each other. Photographs were taken. Speeches were made. Our French friends performed their traditional cross-dressing entertainment before stunned

English onlookers. Dodgy uncles tried to cop a feel of any unguarded boobs. Everyone drank copious amounts of alcohol.

Martine is to be seen on every photo taken after 7pm with both thumbs in the air and a vodka-fuelled manic grin on her face. When we did our first dance to 'La Chanson' by Claude Nougaro, chosen for its shortness, I had to hold her fast to stop her from spiralling recklessly across the floor and I whispered, 'Stay with me baby.'

She looked at me with tears of joy in her eyes and I knew she always would.

Martine and Deborah - May 27th 2006

Postscript: Bert (II)

A few years ago, as I approached my fiftieth birthday, I decided I'd like to know more about my real father, Bert. I had a memory of seeing a small article in the local paper about his death, so I went to the town library to set about finding it.

Hours of searching proved useless. I feared I had got the date of his death wrong, or that the memory of the elusive article had been false. So I shifted my search to the local Register of Electors to see when he'd disappeared from the list. I knew his address because my Mum had visited him there when his wife was away. She'd described it as a posh apartment with a grand piano, where he'd sat and played Beethoven to her.

I was right about the date. He had appeared in 1966 but was no longer listed the following year. His wife, Nola, was listed alongside him. Out of curiosity, I wondered how long she'd survived him. I checked a register in each decade since and there she still appeared right up to the most recent edition. She was still alive.

In a crazy madcap decision of breath-taking nerve I decided to pay her a visit. I knocked on the door and was answered in due course by a handsome looking woman in her nineties. I made up a story about being a social scientist in a college (this much was true) carrying out research on French refugees who'd set up home in Northampton after the war. She looked puzzled and explained to me that her husband was not French but Silesian, though he spoke several languages fluently, including French.

She was clearly very happy to talk about her long-dead husband and invited me into her apartment for coffee. There I spent the next hour learning about my father, though much of his life, as he designed, remains shrouded in mystery.

He was born into a wealthy Jewish family in 1906 in Silesia, a country which no longer exists but was partly in Germany and partly Poland. He was a professor of Law and Philosophy and educated at the University of Heidelberg. During the 1930's he had joined a Nazi resistance movement and was involved in operations dropping anti-Nazi leaflets across Czechoslovakia. In 1938 he was captured by the Gestapo and imprisoned. When war broke out he was to be transferred to Auschwitz, but wealth and education had provided him with likeminded friends in influential positions. One of these friends arranged for him to be removed from the transport truck. The order was given for Bert, naked and freezing, to be dropped at a roadside. Here he waited all night for his friend to pick him up. The friend remained true to his word and the two crossed the border out of Germany.

Bert made his way to Paris, where he played piano in a film theatre and worked with the French Resistance. When the Nazis occupied Paris, Bert got out of France and went to Edinburgh where he worked on the land and met his future bride, Nola. He took her name when they married. They had two children.

Bert had led a strange married life—sometimes disappearing for weeks and months at a time, yet still coming back to his job at the ministry of agriculture. There were gaps in the story that even his wife was unable to fill. Nola showed me into the living room and there stood the grand piano just as my mother had described, and on it, a picture of Bert and Nola taken in Tel Aviv just three days before he died. As I held it, I became aware of her studying me closely, and I quickly handed it back to her. The physical resemblance was evident and the last thing I wanted to do was disrupt this kind old lady's memories. I reiterated the purpose of my fictitious thesis, thanked her for her gracious welcome and left.

When I got back to my car I burst into tears and this time I cried for loss—for the father I did not know, and for the puzzling genetic affinities I felt with him that would never, like so much in life, be fathomed.

******

Thanks to **Jamie Delan**o, for technical help and encouragement. And to **Martine Bourdeau**, for all her love and support.

Addendum:

Same-sex marriage was made legal in the UK on March 29, 2014.

A few names have been changed and images obscured in this edition to protect the emotionally fragile.

Cover design: Lepus Books | lepusbooks.co.uk
Cover image © Deborah Delano

Deborah Delano lives near Hebden Bridge in West Yorkshire with her partner, Martine, and a talkative cat called Missie. They won't be getting married as 'it's a profoundly patriarchal institution'. Deborah has just completed writing her debut novel, **"The Saddest Sound"**.

Early praise for **"The Saddest Sound"**

"I started this book as a favour and I finished it as a compulsion. Deborah Delano, in her strikingly sure-footed debut, brings a fresh contemporary female voice to English Crime. Compassionately observed characters, an insightful grasp of period and landscape, and a fine touch with the dreadful and unsettling conspire to make THE SADDEST SOUND the most involving novel of its kind that you will read this year. An impressive introduction to an impressive new author."
Alan Moore – *Watchmen, V for Vendetta, Voice of the Fire*

"Arsey lesbian prossies combine with loveable radfems to reclaim 1980s northern British streets from the predatory overshadowing of a misogynistic killer. A moving and authentic story of female grit and resistance to violence told with insight, candour and humour. Recommended."
A. William James (aka **Jamie Delano**) – *Book Thirteen, Leepus: Dizzy, Hellblazer*

"A thrilling and genuinely frightening debut novel; I read it in one greedy sitting."
Jude Ramsdale – *Assistant head teacher*

"Every so often a book jemmies into a genre, breaking it open to replace the worn mechanisms and follies of the old form while establishing afresh the possibility of a greater truth lying within. Deborah Delano's THE SADDEST SOUND does this to the house of detective fiction...and it's about time."
Alistair Fruish – *Kiss My ASBO*

"A dark novel set in the gritty north, THE SADDEST SOUND reminds us that homophobia, prejudice and poverty are not as distant-past as we think. Grabs you right to the end."
Jan Stevenson – *Web Designer*

www.ingramcontent.com/pod-product-compliance
Ingram Content Group UK Ltd.
Pitfield, Milton Keynes, MK11 3LW, UK
UKHW020419250726
13967UKWH00007B/2714

9 780957 253568